21-DAY FAITH FAST
BELIEVE BEYOND NORMAL LIMITS

21-DAY FAITH FAST
BELIEVE BEYOND NORMAL LIMITS

DAISY S. DANIELS

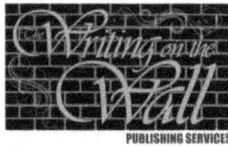

THE WRITING ON THE WALL PUBLISHING SERVICES
ORLANDO, FL 32862, U.S.A.

Unless otherwise indicated, all Scriptural quotations are taken from the *Holy Bible,* New Living Translation, copyright © 1996, 2004. Used by permission of Tyndale House Publishers, Inc., Wheaton, Illinois 60189. Scripture taken from the HOLY BIBLE, NEW INTERNATIONAL VERSION ®. Copyright © 1973, 1978, 1984 by International Bible Society. Used by permission of Zondervan. Scripture quotations marked KJV are from The Full Life Study Bible, King James Version Copyright © 1992 by Life Publishers International

21-DAY FAITH FAST *Believe Beyond Normal Limits*
Daisy S. Daniels
P.O. Box 621433
Orlando, Florida 32862 – 1433
Website:
www.thewritingonthewal.wix.com/daisysdaniels
E-Mail address: thewritingonthewall@aol.com

Library of Congress Control Number: 2015908504

ISBN 978-0-9914002-4-9

Printed in the United States of America

INTRODUCTION

Allow me to start this endeavor with a secret that no girl wants the world to know: I had gained weight. And it wasn't just five or ten pounds. I said, "I had *gained* weight." So anyone who has ever *gained* weight knows what I mean. Anyway, I became a little disappointed with the weight gain, needless to say.

One day, just when I put the potato chip in my mouth, not even all the way in my mouth, on my lip actually, before I was even able to chew it, **THE LORD SAID, "YOU'RE FEEDING A SPIRITUAL NEED WITH A PHYSICAL RESOURCE."** Then He revealed to me that I was *hungry* in the spirit, but I was feeding myself in the natural. What I was hungry for was in the spirit. It wasn't in the natural. I was hungry for God. I wasn't hungry for food.

At the prompting of the Holy Spirit, I was lead to go on a twenty-one (21) day fast. And immediately, the Lord began to minister to me: **THE INSTRUCTIONS WERE CLEAR.**

SO IN PREPARATION OF THE BLESSING, I HONORED MY COMMITMENT UNTO HIM.

The first day of the fast, I got up, showered, and anointed my body; from the crown of my head to the soles of my feet. And with prayer, I offered myself unto Him as a living sacrifice, holy and acceptable unto Him.

And so, my dear brothers and sisters, I want to say that this twenty-one (21) day fast will not focus on what you eat or drink. You can choose whatever you want as your fast. As for me, however, I would eat only one meal a day at 6 p.m. when my fast ended. Now, because I am a vegetarian, my meal consisted of plant based foods; salad, vegetables, water. And I didn't watch any TV during this time. Absolutely none! So, again, it's up to you and whatever God puts on your heart to be your sacrifice. Amen!?

While this fast is not focused on what you eat or drink, **IT IS FOCUSED ON GOD.**

You see, this fast is unlike any fast that I've done because it will result in a blessing unlike any I've ever received. It was during this time that the Lord revealed He wants Randolph and I both to be *Senior Pastor* of our ministry.

The next day, I woke up to the voice of the Lord telling me, **"STRETCH YOUR FAITH."**

And after my due diligence of, "pressing in" to determine what the Lord was saying, The Lord revealed I didn't have the capacity to receive the blessing He was trying to give to me. Therefore, He instructed me to *stretch my faith. Think bigger. Believe beyond the normal limit.*

So, this wasn't just a fast – this was a **FAITH FAST: TO STRETCH MY FAITH; BELIEVE BEYOND NORMAL LIMITS; INCREASE MY CAPACITY TO RECEIVE. BELIEVE FOR THE IMPOSSIBLE.**

I was amazed to say the least. More in awe, I should say, at the fact that He would tell me to increase my capacity instead of just trying to bless me and I *couldn't* receive; and I just missed out on the blessing. He wanted me to receive the blessing! So in case you didn't know, we serve a **good** God. We serve a God who is in the blessing business! He wants to bless His people! He wants to see His people prosper!

So, I believe that you're reading this book because you, too, want to stretch your faith; believe beyond normal limits. I believe that you, too, want to believe the impossible and receive the invisible.

Therefore, I'm looking forward to us taking this journey together.

I want to suggest, for encouragement, that you read *one day of the words of encouragement* for each day that you're on the twenty-one day fast.

AND WATCH THE LORD INCREASE YOUR FAITH BEYOND THE NORMAL LIMITS.

NOW UNTO HIM THAT IS ABLE TO DO EXCEEDING
ABUNDANTLY ABOVE ALL THAT WE ASK OR THINK,
ACCORDING TO THE POWER THAT WORKETH IN US,

EPHESIANS 3:20 KJV

THE APOSTLES SAID TO THE LORD, "SHOW US HOW TO INCREASE OUR FAITH."

LUKE 17:5 NLT

DAY 1

GOD LOOKS DOWN FROM HEAVEN
ON THE ENTIRE HUMAN RACE;
HE LOOKS TO SEE IF ANYONE IS TRULY WISE,
IF ANYONE SEEKS GOD.

PSALM 53:2 NLT

As the above-mentioned passage of scripture states, God is looking to see if anyone is "truly wise." And by truly wise He means, is anyone seeking Him. Is anyone looking for Him?

Hebrews, chapter eleven, verse six, selection a, tells us that without faith it is impossible to please God. So if we're on a faith fast to believe beyond normal limits, why aren't we looking for God?

WE SHOULD BE LOOKING FOR GOD.

He is looking, watching, to see if we'll come to Him, seek Him for wisdom, for the *thing* that we are *hoping* for; faith.

Therefore, sometimes, and I say this often, in order to receive the blessings of God, it requires us to **actively participate** in receiving the blessings. Or in this case, actively participate in order to receive the faith that we need to believe beyond normal limits.

What do I mean by actively participate? Just as the scripture states: we have to *seek* Him, *look* to Him. And by seeking Him, I mean, *praise* Him and *worship* Him, prayer, *studying* His word, *desire* His presence, *long* for Him.

The primary key to faith, and I can't stress this enough is – in God.

FAITH IN GOD.

So, if you're wise, the first step to increasing your faith is to *seek* Him, *look* to Him. And by seeking Him, I mean, *praise* Him and *worship* Him, prayer, *studying* His word, *desire* His presence, *long* for Him.

Why do I have to praise and worship Him if I want to increase my faith? Doesn't increasing your faith mean to *believe more for the thing that I want?*

Well, I'm glad you asked.

FAITH IS THE FOUNDATION OF OUR RELATIONSHIP WITH GOD.

We believe God exists by faith. We believe He is the only true and living God by faith. We believe we are saved by faith. Therefore, our relationship with God is established by faith – in Him. Faith in Him because we believe He has given us a measure of faith; faith in Him because He saved us by His grace – through faith. Our faith in Him believes He is who He says He is. Our faith in Him believes He does just what He says He'll do. Our faith in Him believes He keeps His promises.

And consequently, if we don't have a relationship with God, we don't have faith. And as I mentioned above, if you don't have faith it is impossible to please God – from whom all blessings flow.

ANYONE WHO WANTS TO COME TO HIM MUST BELIEVE THAT GOD EXISTS AND THAT HE REWARDS THOSE WHO SINCERELY SEEK HIM.

HEBREWS 11:6B NLT

I'd like to point out that the King James Version of this scripture reference states:

...he is a rewarder of them that diligently seek him.

So if we seek God *diligently,* seek God *earnestly, wholeheartedly,* He will reward us.

Now that's *not* to say that every time we *seek* Him – *look* to Him, *praise* Him and *worship* Him, *prayer, studying* His word, *desire* His presence, *long* for Him – that He'll bless us with a new "this, that, or the other." It simply means that you will not leave His presence and not be blessed in the manner in which He sees fit to bless you.

IT IS A BLESSING IN ITSELF JUST TO BE IN
HIS PRESENCE. EVERYONE CAN'T COME INTO THE
PRESENCE OF THE LORD. SO YOU SHOULD BE
HONORED.

I also want to point out that just believing that God exists doesn't in itself establish our relationship. Our relationship with God is no different than any other relationship that we have. We have to develop it, build it, nurture it, pay attention to it, cultivate it – get personal. Casting our care and dependence on Him because He cares for us; He supplies our every need; He wants us to put our trust in Him.

Now, with that being said, I want to share with you my twenty-one day faith fast. I started with praise and worship. As I worshiped the Lord, the vision was before me:

IN A VISION...

I saw someone climbing a mountain.

I understood this mountain to be a **MOUNTAIN OF FAITH.**

THE LORD SAID,

"YOU ARE NEARING THE TOP OF THE MOUNTAIN. YOU ARE COMING INTO YOUR GLORY. IT HAS BEEN TOUGH, BUT YOU ARE GOING TO MAKE IT."

You've been trusting. You've been believing. You've been hoping. And you're wondering if it's going to happen. Well, I'm here to tell you that it *will* happen. And sooner than you think! Because you are closer than you think!

AND LET US NOT GROW WEARY OF DOING GOOD, FOR IN DUE SEASON WE WILL REAP, IF WE DO NOT GIVE UP.

GALATIANS 6:9 ESV

Allow me to share with you why *"the climb"* is so difficult. God is trying to get you to stretch your faith. He is trying to bless you with far more than you are expecting, far more than you are believing for; far more than you are hoping for; and far more than you can even imagine.

And in order for Him to make good on His promise to bless you, exceedingly, abundantly above all that you can ask for or think of, you have to make room for the promise. You have to make room for the blessing **BY FAITH.**

Before He allows you to miss this blessing, He'll keep you on the mountain, stretching you and stretching your faith until you have room enough to receive it.

HE'S NOT GOING TO LET YOU MISS THIS BLESSING.

- ❖ Before He allows you to miss this blessing, He would change His plans for your life.
- ❖ Before He allows you to miss this blessing, He would change His purpose for your life.
- ❖ Before He allows you to miss this blessing, He would change His will for your life.
- ❖ Before He allows you to miss this blessing, He would change your destiny.

That's how much He wants to bless you. But guess what – **HE'S NOT GOING TO DO THAT!**

- ❖ HE'S NOT GOING TO CHANGE HIS PLANS
- ❖ HE'S NOT GOING TO CHANGE HIS PURPOSE
- ❖ HE'S NOT GOING TO CHANGE HIS WILL
- ❖ HE'S NOT GOING TO CHANGE YOUR DESTINY

HE'S GOING TO STRETCH YOU BEYOND YOUR LIMITS.

Then suddenly the Lord revealed to me:

IN A VISION...

I saw an astronaut just floating in space.

Immediately I understood that the person couldn't find their way and they felt all alone. You're just going along with the flow – "whatever happens happens" attitude.

THE LORD SAID,

"CHANGE YOUR ATTITUDE, AND YOU'LL SEE HIM WORK IN YOUR LIFE."

No more just going along with the flow. No more just going along with the program. No more *just enough to get by.* No more "whatever happens happens" attitude.

ACTIVATE YOUR FAITH.

GOD'S GOT YOU.

THE FATHER INSTANTLY CRIED OUT, "I DO
BELIEVE, BUT HELP ME OVERCOME MY UNBELIEF!"

MARK 9:24 NLT

DAY 2

BUT THEY THAT WAIT UPON THE LORD SHALL
RENEW THEIR STRENGTH; THEY SHALL MOUNT UP
WITH WINGS AS EAGLES; THEY SHALL RUN, AND
NOT BE WEARY; AND THEY SHALL WALK, AND
NOT FAINT.

ISAIAH 40:31 KJV

Let me start by saying, there are a number of ways that I use the term "wait upon the Lord" in order to describe what it means to "wait upon the Lord." In doing so, "waiting upon the Lord," I am assured that the Lord will give me everything that I need to take my faith to the next level – in Him.

Now, more often than not, the term that is used to describe *wait upon the Lord* is: TO SERVE THE LORD. While you are "waiting" on the Lord to bless you, you should serve Him. Just like you are served by a waiter in a restaurant, you, too, should become a "waiter," unto the Lord, and serve Him while you're waiting upon the Lord. To serve Him means, your focus is on God. He's the only one that you see. He's the only one that you're concerned about. He's the only one that you're trying to please.

To serve Him means you anticipate *His needs:* You rise early in the morning to seek Him. You praise and worship Him for who He is and for His goodness; you honor Him with the fruit of your lips. You meditate on His Word day and night. Your prayer is consistent and focused; you pray in your most holy faith, you pray in tongues; your heavenly language. You fast to help you center your focus on God. I mean, you pull out all the stops. And just like a waiter at a restaurant, it is at His good pleasure that you serve. I mean, you're so good to Him that He'll say, "I'm going to give them a *good* tip, more than the fifteen percent!" Another expression of "wait upon the Lord" that I'd like to use is: YOU STAY IN THE PLACE OF EXPECTATION.

I WILL CLIMB UP TO MY WATCHTOWER
AND STAND AT MY GUARDPOST.
THERE I WILL WAIT TO SEE WHAT THE LORD

SAYS
AND HOW HE WILL ANSWER MY COMPLAINT.

THEN THE LORD SAID TO ME,

"WRITE MY ANSWER PLAINLY ON TABLETS,
SO THAT A RUNNER CAN CARRY THE CORRECT
MESSAGE TO OTHERS.
THIS VISION IS FOR A FUTURE TIME.
IT DESCRIBES THE END, AND IT WILL BE
FULFILLED.
IF IT SEEMS SLOW IN COMING, WAIT PATIENTLY,
FOR IT WILL SURELY TAKE PLACE.
IT WILL NOT BE DELAYED.

HABAKKUK 2: 1 – 3 NLT

As I wait upon the Lord, I have His Word, His promise that the vision, the blessing, the *thing* that I hope for will come to pass. And I'm encouraged in His presence as I continue to wait on the promise. I'm strengthened in His presence as I continue to wait on His promise. Although it seems to be slow in coming, I'm mindful that it's for an **appointed time.** It's for a time in the future. And while I wait, I continue to believe. I continue to hope. I continue to fast and pray. I continue to meditate on His Word day and night. I continue to pray in my most holy faith by speaking in tongues. I continue to stand guard. I continue to be the watchman on the wall – **EXPECTING, WAITING, LOOKING** for the promise. Oh, make no mistake – **IT WILL SURELY TAKE PLACE. IT WILL NOT BE DELAYED.**

And yet, another expression of "wait upon the Lord" I like to use to describe what it means to *wait upon the Lord* is: **TO CALL UPON THE LORD.** To call upon the Lord means that *I cry out to Him* to help me in my times of trouble, testing, and/or suffering. I look to Him to help me when I can't make it on my own. It means that when I've done all that I can do to stand, I'm able to call on Him and He'll take me the rest of the way – until the battle is won.

To call upon the Lord means that I'm able to go boldly before His throne to receive His mercy in my time of need. Whether I'm suffering, tormented, weak, in anguish, and/or need to be comforted, He gives me the grace that I need to endure. Whether I'm struggling with fear, doubt, worry, confusion, apprehension, and/or losing hope, He gives me the grace that I need to endure.

THIS HIGH PRIEST OF OURS UNDERSTANDS OUR WEAKNESSES, FOR HE FACED ALL OF THE SAME TESTINGS WE DO, YET HE DID NOT SIN. SO LET US COME BOLDLY TO THE THRONE OF OUR GRACIOUS GOD. THERE WE WILL RECEIVE HIS MERCY, AND WE WILL FIND GRACE TO HELP US WHEN WE NEED IT MOST.

HEBREWS 4:15 – 16 NLT

Now, as I continued to seek the Lord, He revealed to me:

IN A VISION...

I saw God sitting on the throne. And immediately, I was prompted to worship Him.

Surprisingly, I couldn't get the CD player or the MP3 player to work, so I started to sing unto Him – **OUT OF MY BELLY FLOWED RIVERS OF LIVING WATERS.** Whatever He prompted me to sing, I sung. At His leading, at His prompting, I worshipped Him.

HE THAT BELIEVETH ON ME, AS THE SCRIPTURE
HATH SAID, OUT OF HIS BELLY SHALL FLOW
RIVERS OF LIVING WATER.

JOHN 7:38 KJV

As the rivers of living waters flowed from my belly, I continued to worship the Lord. And the tears started to stream down my face because of His presence. The tears continued to flow down my face as I was reminded that He reigns. He sits on the throne. He reigns. With all power, He reigns. With all authority, He reigns. And as I loved on Him, He loved on me.

MY ONLY FOCUS WAS TO WORSHIP HIM.

ACKNOWLEDGE THAT THE LORD IS GOD!
HE MADE US, AND WE ARE HIS.
WE ARE HIS PEOPLE, THE SHEEP OF HIS PASTURE.
ENTER HIS GATES WITH THANKSGIVING;
GO INTO HIS COURTS WITH PRAISE.
GIVE THANKS TO HIM AND PRAISE HIS NAME.
FOR THE LORD IS GOOD.
HIS UNFAILING LOVE CONTINUES FOREVER,
AND HIS FAITHFULNESS CONTINUES TO EACH
GENERATION.

PSALM 100:3 – 5 NLT

And in the midst of me worshiping Him, the Lord revealed to me:

IN A VISION...

I saw an eagle, soaring.

And immediately, I understood that I was being strengthened. And although I had been overwhelmed with life's frailties, the Lord was strengthening me. At His prompting, at His unction, I came to get what I didn't know I needed; His grace to endure.

The soaring eagle is a representation of someone rising above the difficulties that they face. Just like the eagle uses the wind beneath his wings to soar, without any effort, *we* have to put our trust in the Lord so that He'll make it possible for us to soar – without any effort of our own. Now that I had been strengthened I could face the difficulties, head on.

❖ The soaring eagle represents God giving us the ability to run spiritually and not get weary.

❖ The soaring eagle represents God giving us the ability to walk spiritually and not faint.

The Lord was enabling me to do what He has called me to do. And as I continue to trust Him, He'll continue to sustain me.

THE LORD SAID,

"THE HEARTS OF THE PEOPLE ARE PURE BEFORE ME."

The Lord sees your heart. Therefore, I just want to encourage you today. He knows what you need. Allow Him to give you what you need. If you're expecting God to do something for you that you can't do for yourself; if you want faith that believes beyond the normal limits – *get in the Lord's presence.* The Lord has been prompting you to praise Him. He has been prompting you to worship Him. Don't ignore His promptings. Don't ignore His invitation. Follow the prompting of His Holy Spirit. Serve the Lord with gladness! Bless Him in His holy temple.

And you'll find that everything you need is in His presence.

"YOU DON'T HAVE ENOUGH FAITH," JESUS TOLD
THEM. "I TELL YOU THE TRUTH, IF YOU HAD
FAITH EVEN AS SMALL AS A MUSTARD SEED, YOU
COULD SAY TO THIS MOUNTAIN, 'MOVE FROM HERE
TO THERE,' AND IT WOULD MOVE. NOTHING
WOULD BE IMPOSSIBLE."

MATTHEW 17:20 NLT

DAY 3

I WILL BLESS THE LORD AT ALL TIMES: HIS PRAISE
SHALL CONTINUALLY BE IN MY MOUTH.

PSALM 34:1 KJV

There is one thing that we can be assured of,
and that is, there is power in the name of Jesus! I
said there is POWER in the name of Jesus!
Therefore, let us...

Exalt the name of our Lord and Savior –
Jesus!

When I talk about the power in the name of
Jesus, I'm talking about the power that heals the
sick, raises the dead. I'm talking about the power
that causes the blind to see or the deaf to hear. And
I'm talking about the power that causes the lame to
walk or the mute to speak. The power of Jesus
encompasses all of these expressions. Now I want
to talk about another expression of His power.

I'm talking about the power that gives us the ability to do something or to act. The power, the ability for you to do what the Lord called you to do. The power, the ability is in the name of Jesus. So if you're struggling with believing God for the blessing that is beyond the normal limit, call on the name of Jesus! And He'll give you the power, ability to believe.

THE ABILITY TO BELIEVE; THE ABILITY TO STRETCH YOUR FAITH – IS IN THE NAME OF JESUS!

Therefore, allow me to encourage you today to *use the power* that's in the name of Jesus. Well, let me say it this way, it's *your faith in GOD'S ability to get it done.* But you use the power by trusting that He is going to do it. So, if it's faith that you lack, let your prayer become:

LORD, GIVE ME THE FAITH, THE CONFIDENCE THAT I NEED TO BELIEVE AND EXPECT YOU TO DO WHAT YOU SAID YOU WOULD DO.

Again, and I can't stress this enough, your confidence, power, and ability comes as a result of believing *in* God. It is not in anything else or anyone else. Believe in the Lord, Jesus Christ and you shall recover all.

Use the power and the authority that's in the name of Jesus to accomplish what you're trying to accomplish, which is to increase your faith to believe Him for the impossible.

As I called on the name of the Lord, the Lord revealed to me:

IN A VISION...

I saw the "destroying angel" a "warring angel".

And immediately afterwards, I saw the face of a demon.

THE LORD SAID,

"THE ENEMY IS BEING DESTROYED."

'VENGEANCE IS MINE, AND RECOMPENSE,
FOR THE TIME WHEN THEIR FOOT SHALL SLIP;
FOR THE DAY OF THEIR CALAMITY IS AT HAND,
AND THEIR DOOM COMES SWIFTLY.'

DEUTERONOMY 32:35 ESV

Trust in the Lord. Trust in His ability to do it. Trust Him to defeat the enemies that are coming against you; that are trying to hold you back; that are trying to keep you from doing what God has called you to do; that are trying to keep you from advancing to the next level. Whatever demon you're struggling with:

❖ Fear, Worry, Doubt, Confusion,
Concern, Hesitation, Uncertainty,
Disbelief, Insecurity, Wavering Faith,
Lack of confidence in God, Lack of self-
confidence, Anxiety…

Whatever it is, the Lord is destroying it today! Declare your victory on today. The enemy that you see today you will see no more. Stand firm and see the salvation of the Lord!

I heard the Lord saying, "The enemy is being destroyed." This may even be a "lying spirit" that's causing you to think that whatever you're believing for won't happen. It's being destroyed today!

Speak to those things that concern you. Speak to the worry and doubt, and begin to speak the word of God over those things. Declare your victory over those things!

Remember, there is power in the name of Jesus! Power is His ability to do something or to act. In other words, I have the ability to defeat the enemy because of the name of Jesus! So, when I call on the name of Jesus, it gives me power. I have the ability to do what He has called me to do. I have the ability to act on what He has told me to do. I have the ability; I have the power to believe I can take the next step.

THAT POWER...IS FAITH.

I have the faith to do what I believe the Lord has called me to do. As long as I believe in the name of Jesus, I can do all things that He strengthens me to do. I can do all things that He has called me to do. The power, faith to do it is in the name of Jesus.

So be a part of what God is doing in your life. Act on your faith, act by faith so that you can receive the blessings of the Lord. Therefore, we have to believe by faith, by praising Him for it. For whatever you need. Don't forget to...

Use the power that's in the name of Jesus. It's *your faith in HIS ability to get it done.*

And if you are lacking in faith, if you are not as confident in His ability to do just what He said He would do, call on the name of Jesus: "Lord, give me the confidence that I need to believe that YOU are going to do what You said You would do. Amen."

HEN JESUS TOLD THEM, "I TELL YOU THE TRUTH, IF YOU HAVE FAITH AND DON'T DOUBT, YOU CAN DO THINGS LIKE THIS AND MUCH MORE. YOU CAN EVEN SAY TO THIS MOUNTAIN, 'MAY YOU BE LIFTED UP AND THROWN INTO THE SEA,' AND IT WILL HAPPEN.

MATTHEW 21:21 NLT

DAY 4

BUT JESUS SAID, "YOU FEED THEM."

LUKE 9:13 NLT

We know the story…

LATE IN THE AFTERNOON THE TWELVE DISCIPLES CAME TO HIM AND SAID, "SEND THE CROWDS AWAY TO THE NEARBY VILLAGES AND FARMS, SO THEY CAN FIND FOOD AND LODGING FOR THE NIGHT. THERE IS NOTHING TO EAT HERE IN THIS REMOTE PLACE."

BUT JESUS SAID, "YOU FEED THEM."

"BUT WE HAVE ONLY FIVE LOAVES OF BREAD AND TWO FISH," THEY ANSWERED. "OR ARE YOU EXPECTING US TO GO AND BUY ENOUGH FOOD FOR THIS WHOLE CROWD?" FOR THERE WERE ABOUT 5,000 MEN THERE.

JESUS REPLIED, "TELL THEM TO SIT DOWN IN GROUPS OF ABOUT FIFTY EACH." SO THE PEOPLE ALL SAT DOWN. JESUS TOOK THE FIVE LOAVES AND TWO FISH, LOOKED UP TOWARD HEAVEN, AND BLESSED THEM. THEN, BREAKING THE LOAVES INTO PIECES, HE KEPT GIVING THE BREAD AND FISH TO THE DISCIPLES SO THEY COULD DISTRIBUTE IT TO THE PEOPLE. THEY ALL ATE AS MUCH AS THEY WANTED, AND AFTERWARD, THE

DISCIPLES PICKED UP TWELVE BASKETS OF LEFTOVERS!

LUKE 9:12 – 17 NLT

THE LORD SAID,

"FEED YOUR FAITH."

What does it mean to feed your faith?

Just as the above passage of scriptures reflect, feeding your faith means you have to *do something to satisfy the need.* When the people got hungry, instead of sending them away, Jesus fed them. And the same holds true for us in stretching our faith. When we get to a place where we are *hungry in the spirit,* we have to feed that need. And the way we feed it is with faith, which means we have to *do something to satisfy the need, the hunger.*

Do something that is going to encourage you in your faith. Do something that is going to strengthen your faith, build up your faith. Do something that's going to give you the confidence you need to take that next step.

I know it may seem impossible to do what needs to be done in order to take the next step of faith, but it's crucial that you do it. If you don't feed your faith, you will become faint:

"I FEEL SORRY FOR THESE PEOPLE. THEY HAVE BEEN HERE WITH ME FOR THREE DAYS, AND THEY HAVE NOTHING LEFT TO EAT. IF I SEND THEM HOME HUNGRY, THEY WILL FAINT ALONG THE WAY. FOR SOME OF THEM HAVE COME A LONG DISTANCE."

MARK 8:2 – 3 NLT

And I know you, just like these people, have come too far to faint now.

Taking the next step may in fact seem overwhelming, maybe not 5,000 overwhelming, but still, just as overwhelming. This is a new level of faith for you; therefore, it's okay to be a little intimidated, but take the step – intimidation and all.

DO IT.

Now the one thing we can count on, as the above passage of scriptures state, God isn't going to just let you leave. He cares about you. He's not going to let you faint. He's going to make sure you have what you need so that you can be strengthened to make the journey. He's going to feed you, spiritually. He's going to feed you; your need (whatever it is that you need, He's going to give it to you). You see, he's got a lot invested in you. He believes in you.

Take that next step of faith.

While it may be your desire to just let it be, God is not going to allow that to happen. He's not going to let you just give up. He didn't bring you this far for you not to take the next step. You see, the next step will propel you, push you to *believing beyond the normal limits.*

Welcome the change. Greet the fear with faith. Get acquainted with this next level of faith.

Do it.

Take one step at a time. Devote yourself to taking the next step. Don't let the day end without taking that next step. Be it a small step, it's a step.

It's one step closer to receiving all that God has for you in this season.

By taking the next step, by feeding your faith, you'll be satisfying your hunger. You'll be satisfying your desire to get to your destiny; believe beyond normal limits.

JUST LIKE READING FEEDS THE INTELLECT, ACTION FEEDS FAITH.

How do I feed my faith?

You follow the example that Jesus gives us:

JESUS REPLIED, "TELL THEM TO SIT DOWN IN GROUPS OF ABOUT FIFTY EACH." SO THE PEOPLE ALL SAT DOWN. JESUS TOOK THE FIVE LOAVES AND TWO FISH, LOOKED UP TOWARD HEAVEN, AND BLESSED THEM. THEN, BREAKING THE LOAVES INTO PIECES, HE KEPT GIVING THE BREAD AND FISH TO THE DISCIPLES SO THEY COULD DISTRIBUTE IT TO THE PEOPLE. THEY ALL ATE AS MUCH AS THEY WANTED, AND AFTERWARD, THE DISCIPLES PICKED UP TWELVE BASKETS OF LEFTOVERS!

❖ You do it in small groups:

  ○ Or shall I say, little by
    little, step by step. Small
    steps, one step at a time.

❖ Give it to God, and He'll bless
  you:

  ○ Take your insecurity,
    look up toward heaven,
    and give it to God. He
    will bless your insecurity
    with a confident
    expectation – faith, which
    will enable you to take
    that next step.

❖ Then break the faith into pieces:

  ○ Believe that you can
    conquer the first step you
    take. Then believe that
    you can conquer the next
    step you'll take. As you
    take steps, you'll be
    building your faith. You

don't have to do everything at once. Do a little of this, then a little of that, even a little every day until you've accomplished it.

❖ Keep taking steps until you've satisfied your need:

    o Keep doing it until you're full. Keep doing it until you feel comfortable with how the next level of faith works. Keep doing it until you feel like you got a grasp of what the next step is about.

NOW I HAVE TO TELL YOU THAT...THERE WILL BE LEFTOVERS.

Because in essence, what you'll be doing is establishing a track record for God; a track record of God proving Himself to you; a track record of you finding Him faithful. You'll be developing your relationship with God. And when you get to the next level of faith, all you have to do is look back and grab some of the *leftovers.*

The leftovers are a representation of the things God did for you, and how He brought you through. How you made it over. How He made a way when there was no way. How He opened doors where there were no doors. How He did what people said could not be done.

You trusted Him.

Taking the next step will challenge your faith.

Taking the next step will reveal, uncover any hidden things that may be preventing you from walking by faith, like doubt or unbelief. And as these things are revealed, you can give them to God to conquer them.

My simplest prayer concerning a lack of faith is: "Lord, I believe. Help my unbelief."

And not only does He help you, but He gives you the victory. Maybe you're not as confident as you think. Maybe you don't believe as much as you *think* you do. Maybe your faith is not in *God* as much as it is in the *thing* you're hoping for.

HAVE FAITH IN GOD.

God is doing a new thing, and…

It's on another level.

BUT WHEN YOU ASK HIM, BE SURE THAT YOUR
FAITH IS IN GOD ALONE. DO NOT WAVER, FOR A
PERSON WITH DIVIDED LOYALTY IS AS UNSETTLED
AS A WAVE OF THE SEA THAT IS BLOWN AND
TOSSED BY THE WIND.

JAMES 1:6 NLT

DAY 5

AND ELISHA SAID, I PRAY THEE, LET A DOUBLE PORTION OF THY SPIRIT BE UPON ME.

2 KINGS 2:9B KJV

As soon as I sat down in my secret place, my spirit began singing unto the Lord. I wasn't surprised. As I slept, I was awakened by the Lord inviting me to praise Him; I was awakened with a song in my spirit. I sat quietly to hear the song. As soon as I heard the words, I began singing the song that rung out in my spirit. Whatever my spirit sung, I sung. Whatever melody I heard in my spirit was the melody that I sung.

I stood before the Lord worshiping Him as my spirit dictated. I anticipated the Lord's presence. I was expecting the Lord's presence as I continued to sing to Him. As I continued to sing before Him, I started to sense His presence ever so slightly, but I knew He was there.

I continued to honor Him as I stood before His throne. Then the spirit took over. I started singing in tongues; my heavenly language. I couldn't help but wonder what my spirit was singing. I wanted to know the interpretation. And was comforted in believing my spirit was singing the same song because the melody had not changed. But I didn't know for sure.

And immediately, the Lord made His presence known as the anointing weighed heavily on my head, and my spirit began to weaken. The tears started to roll down my face. I felt myself swaying as the power of His Holy Spirit rested upon me. And as I continued to sing in tongues, I knew something was about to happen.

As I worshipped, the Lord revealed to me:

IN A VISION:

I saw a girl in her graduation cap and gown. And I saw a hand on a globe.

Immediately, I knew she had graduated, and she was about to step out into the world.

I continued to sing before the Lord as He continued to minister to me.

THE LORD SAID,

"DOUBLE PORTION."

And I started to praise Him all the more as I was excited in my spirit about the blessing. I received it, and began to weep before Him all the more. And He continued.

THE LORD SAID,

"TELL MY PEOPLE, A DOUBLE PORTION; FOR THOSE WHO BELIEVE, A DOUBLE PORTION NOW; TODAY."

And instantly, unable to continue to stand, I fell to my knees, and bowed before Him. I wept loudly. I cried out before Him as my spirit continued to worship Him; Honoring Him.

And then I saw Him leave.

**GOD HAD COME DOWN OFF HIS THRONE
TO BLESS HIS PEOPLE. MY GOD!**

I continued to weep.

After somewhat getting myself together, I was excited and anxious to tell the people what *thus said the Lord.* But I was unable to get up. His anointing was still heavy upon me, and I couldn't get up; I couldn't leave His presence. So I continued to sit before Him. His Words continued to ring out in my spirit, and I continued to weep.

Then, the anointing lifted.

A DOUBLE PORTION.

For those of us who've graduated at any point in our life, whether it was kindergarten, grade school, junior high school, high school, college, grad school, or post grad, we understand that graduation is, for the most part, a very significant milestone. Graduation is an indication that we're getting ready to embark on a new chapter in our lives; the end of one chapter, and the beginning of a new. It signifies I have completed my course. It's a sign of maturity; a knowledgeable and teachable student. And it propels us to move forward; whatever that path may be, and wherever it may lead. We follow.

Well, today is no different. **TODAY IS GRADUATION DAY!**

YOU HAVE REACHED YET ANOTHER SIGNIFICANT MILESTONE IN YOUR LIFE. YOU'RE GETTING READY TO EMBARK ON A NEW CHAPTER. YOU HAVE COMPLETED YOUR COURSE. YOU'VE MATURED. YOU'RE KNOWLEDGEABLE AND TEACHABLE. AND NOW...IT'S TIME TO MOVE FORWARD. WHATEVER PATH THAT MAY BE. AND WHEREVER THAT PATH MAY LEAD YOU...FOLLOW IT.

THE INTERPRETATION OF THE VISION...

The hand in the vision is the hand of God. And it represents His divine power.

And the globe represents going out into the world.

YOU ARE ABOUT TO GO OUT INTO THE WORLD WITH GOD'S DIVINE POWER.

Now, I must tell you that going out into the world means you are about to start ministry.

So, let me say it this way: **YOU ARE ABOUT TO GO INTO MINISTRY BY THE HAND OF GOD AND WITH HIS DIVINE POWER.**

You've studied. You've been trained. You've passed the test. And now…it's graduation day!

AND IT CAME TO PASS, WHEN THEY WERE GONE OVER, THAT ELIJAH SAID UNTO ELISHA, ASK WHAT I SHALL DO FOR THEE, BEFORE I BE TAKEN AWAY FROM THEE. AND ELISHA SAID, I PRAY THEE, LET A DOUBLE PORTION OF THY SPIRIT BE UPON ME.

2 KINGS 2:9 KJV

You've been fasting. You've been praying. You've been hoping. You've been believing.

"YOU HAVE ASKED A DIFFICULT THING," ELIJAH REPLIED. "IF YOU SEE ME WHEN I AM TAKEN FROM YOU, THEN YOU WILL GET YOUR REQUEST. BUT IF NOT, THEN YOU WON'T."

AS THEY WERE WALKING ALONG AND TALKING, SUDDENLY A CHARIOT OF FIRE APPEARED, DRAWN BY HORSES OF FIRE. IT DROVE BETWEEN THE TWO MEN, SEPARATING THEM, AND ELIJAH WAS CARRIED BY A WHIRLWIND INTO HEAVEN. ELISHA SAW IT AND CRIED OUT, "MY FATHER! MY FATHER! I SEE THE CHARIOTS AND CHARIOTEERS OF ISRAEL!" AND AS THEY DISAPPEARED FROM SIGHT, ELISHA TORE HIS CLOTHES IN DISTRESS.

2 KINGS 2:10 – 12 NLT

The Lord is saying to you TODAY that the double portion is not *if* you believe. He said, '*for* those who believe.' The double portion is *for* those who believe. Let me say it this way:

You have been blessed with a double portion! A double portion of His Spirit!

You have already received it! *Because* you believe! My God! The Lord has **already** given the double portion to you! Not *if* you believe – *because* you believe!

The Lord has just answered your prayer! He has just granted your request!

You already have it! He already gave it to you!

So what am I saying?

The double portion of His Spirit *is* the increased capacity that we've believed for in order to receive the blessings that He has for us. And He has answered our prayer. He has granted our request. He has given us what we've been praying for, fasting for, hoping for, believing for…an increased capacity to believe.

FAITH…BEYOND THE NORMAL LIMITS.

And just like Elisha, he received the double portion because he believed.

You are reading this book because right here, right **NOW, TODAY,** you have been blessed with a double portion of the Lord's Spirit.

A DOUBLE PORTION.

"For" you.

BUT JESUS TURNED HIM ABOUT, AND WHEN HE
SAW HER, HE SAID, DAUGHTER, BE OF GOOD
COMFORT; THY FAITH HATH MADE THEE WHOLE.
AND THE WOMAN WAS MADE WHOLE FROM THAT
HOUR.

MATTHEW 9:22 KJV

DAY 6

OPEN THE MOUTH OF THE FIRST FISH YOU CATCH, AND YOU WILL FIND A LARGE SILVER COIN.

MATTHEW 17:27B NLT

My devotion with the Lord extended from 3 a.m. to 7 a.m. then I went back to bed; only to be awakened again at 10 a.m. with a song in my spirit. The Lord was inviting me back into His presence. In obedience to His prompting, I was excited to SEE what He had to say. Immediately, I got up singing the song that was in my spirit as I prepared myself to go before Him.

But the beautiful day outside caught my attention and I stepped out onto the balcony to see the *fish* in the pond. As I stood there looking, I continued to follow the Holy Spirit's lead as I continued to sing unto the Lord. And while there were a couple of fish, it wasn't the *school* of fish I had seen before. Still, I was excited to see them. Now I could finally show or prove to my husband there were fish in the pond. (Because it seemed that every time I tried to show him the fish, they were never there. So of course, me being all "spiritual" and "deep" you know, I figured, he couldn't see the fish because He wasn't looking with his spiritual eyes. *I'm laughing of course.*)

Anyway, I could see there were a couple of fish (and the momma and baby turtle). So as I continued to sing, I called Randolph to come see the fish. Finally! He saw the fish. Not impressed, he walked away. *How could he not be excited?* I wondered. Then I realized the Lord was ministering to me through song, which is why he wasn't excited, but I was. You see, these weren't just "fish" these were fish that represented the lives that were to be saved, the souls that were to be saved to advance God's kingdom. Spiritually, fish represent life.

However, I was determined not to be moved because he wasn't excited. I mean, it had only been *a few days* that I had been trying to show him these fish. So, anyway, I continued to sing unto the Lord. Then all of a sudden, I saw something "large" swimming in the pond. *Oh, my God,* I thought, *it must be a baby alligator.* Florida is known for its alligators. I mean, you never know where they may show up. In someone's back yard, in the swimming pool...wherever! And now one was in our pond. *Oh, Lord!*

Quickly, and excited (now for a different reason), I called my husband to come. There was something "huge" swimming in the pond. "Honey, hurry," I called as whatever it was swam by. "Hurry! Hurry! There's something huge in the pond! Oh, my God!" But of course by the time he made it, there was nothing there to see. Of course! Right? But I stood there, as the song of the Lord continued to ring out in my spirit. "Lord, let me see it again," I prayed.

And from out of nowhere, there it was! It was a "huge" fish. He had to be at least two feet (if not more). I kid you not! "Oh, my God!" I screamed. "There it is! Honey, it's a fish! Oh, my God! Honey, hurry! Come see it!" And just as he came running, it disappeared. "Wait, wait, wait," I said as I encouraged him not to leave.

Immediately, I was excited in my spirit (as you can tell), because as the Lord continued to minister to me, He revealed, the fish was an indication that I had enlarged my capacity to believe for "bigger!" And still, I wanted Randolph to see it! He waited, and ta-dahhhh…the fish appeared. "Oh, my God!" I continued to scream. "Honey, he's got to be about three feet, right?" I questioned. But he said nothing.

Again, seemingly he was not impressed. "Oh, wait! Honey, there's another one! There are two big fish!" I said as the second fish made his debut. But not to be outdone by the second fish, the first comes up out of the water, mouth opened then it quickly snapped closed. He caught something! "Oh, my God," I screamed. And still, not impressed, he walked away. "Honey, wait!" I shouted. "There's a third one! There are three of them!" But he didn't come back. Amazed, not only excited to see the fish, but my spirit was excited about what the Lord had revealed; therefore, I worshiped Him all the more.

My capacity to believe for bigger; to believe for more had been enlarged.

I went into my secret place to focus my attention on the Lord as I worshiped Him. As I was worshiping, I kept seeing the vision of the fish. I couldn't get it out of my mind. In fact, I was a little disturbed in my spirit because *seemingly* I was distracted by the fish. And yet, I continued to worship.

IN A VISION...

There were fish everywhere; fish, fish, and more fish. Far more fish than I had actually seen in the pond. And yet, I continued to try to shake the vision, but it wouldn't leave. So I continued to worship the Lord in song as the Spirit prompted me.

Then suddenly,

IN A VISION...

The fish with the opened mouth that came out of the water was before me.

And immediately, the Lord reminded me of the fish with the coin in his mouth. And instantly, I could see the coin that was in the fish's mouth. And immediately, I began to sing in tongues; in my heavenly language as the Spirit took control of me.

THE LORD SAID,

"**TELL MY PEOPLE I AM THE WAY MAKER. I AM THE HEALER. I AM THE FINANCIAL BREAKTHROUGH. WISDOM IS MINE. I KNOW WHERE THE FISH ARE.**"

By this time, I was prostrate before the Lord.

OPEN THE MOUTH OF THE FIRST FISH YOU CATCH, AND YOU WILL FIND A LARGE SILVER COIN.

MATTHEW 17: 27B NLT

You're probably already familiar with this scripture. And, therefore, you probably already know that the scripture is a reflection of the citizen's duty to pay their taxes. You probably already know that this scripture is a reflection of Christ performing a miracle. You probably already know that this scripture is a reflection of Christ's divine power of nature. And you probably already know that this scripture is a reflection of Christ's divine supply.

However, I want to share with you that while I also understood these same scriptural principles, I knew the Lord was saying something else. This wasn't *just* about paying taxes. This wasn't *just* about a miracle. This wasn't *just* about power over nature. This wasn't *just* about divine supply. So I continued to *press in* so that the Lord would reveal the interpretation, the understanding of what He was saying in the vision.

"...SO GO DOWN TO THE LAKE AND THROW IN A LINE. OPEN THE MOUTH OF THE FIRST FISH YOU CATCH, AND YOU WILL FIND A LARGE SILVER

COIN. TAKE IT AND PAY THE TAX FOR BOTH OF US."

MATTHEW 17:27 NLT

The Lord revealed that THIS was about TWO THINGS:

- ❖ HE IS DEMANDING THAT WE PUT FORTH EFFORT TO GET WHAT HE HAS PROVIDED.
- ❖ HE IS DEMANDING RESULTS FROM THE BLESSINGS THAT HE HAS ENTRUSTED US WITH.

What demand? What effort?

Well, let me say it this way:

The Lord instructed Peter to do several things:

- ❖ Go down to the lake
- ❖ Throw in a line
- ❖ Open the mouth of the first fish you catch
- ❖ Find a large silver coin

❖ Take the coin out of the fish's mouth

❖ Pay the taxes for both of them.

And the result:

❖ Their taxes would be paid, and the tax collectors wouldn't be offended.

And thereby their *duty* was performed, *a miracle* was performed, *power* over nature was performed, and *a divine* supply was performed.

So, while the Lord had provided and met the financial need, in this case, Peter had to put forth effort to get the blessing, the miracle that Jesus had provided and performed. And consequently, He was expecting results; He was expecting Peter to do exactly as He had told him to do in order to get the results that He had provided for him.

You see, God knows where the *fish* are. He knows where your next miracle is. And guess what, He also revealed that He has already told you...where to go to get it; what to do when you get there; what to do with it, and the purpose for it.

However, unlike Peter, we haven't put forth an effort to get the blessing that the Lord is trying to get into our hands. We haven't put forth the effort to get the miracle that He has provided for us. And consequently, He is expecting results from what He has given us; He's expecting results from what He has provided for us. He is expecting us to do exactly as He told us to do in order to get the blessing, the miracle that He has provided for us.

TIME IS OF THE ESSENCE. WE MUST WORK DILIGENTLY. WE MUST WORK WITH A SENSE OF URGENCY; LEST THE FISH DISAPPEARS.

The Lord is trying to get the miracle into our hands. When He says He **KNOWS** where the fish are, He **KNOWS** where your next miracle is. I hate to say it, but...

- ❖ The very place where you don't want to go – that's where the miracle is.
- ❖ The very thing you're afraid of doing – that's what performs the miracle.

❖ The very reason you believe for the fish – that's the purpose of the miracle.

Go! Do it! Have faith!

GOD IS TRYING TO GET A MIRACLE INTO YOUR HANDS!

AND JESUS ANSWERING SAITH UNTO THEM, HAVE FAITH IN GOD.

MARK 11:22 KJV

DAY 7

Every morning I woke up with a song in my spirit and today isn't any different. I lie in bed for a few minutes listening to the song as it played over and over in my spirit. And based on the song that was in my spirit, I started to declare: I'm tired of going around this same ol' mountain. I have had enough!

IN A VISION...

I see this fish of some sort before me. I can't seem to shake the vision. It almost looks like a baby shark, and it appears to be caught or trapped.

I got out of bed, and prepared myself to go before the Lord. As I'm preparing myself and the song is in my spirit, I see my business logo. And something in me started to declare, "I see it. I see it being birthed. I see it being born. I see it coming forth."

I got it! I see the vision happening! It is going to happen! I believe by faith it's going to happen! I believe it! It's going to happen!

In my spirit, I receive it.

And as I stretched, and I mean stretched my hand unto the Lord, immediately, I was reminded of a church service I attended. At this particular service, sitting to the left of me was a gentleman who had to be at least six feet seven inches (at least) and to the left of him was Dwight Howard of the Orlando Magic. It was clear that the young man and Dwight were together. And my son, who was at the time about fourteen years old, was excited that we were sitting next to Dwight Howard. I knew my son would be excited to tell his friends that he had seen Dwight in church, so I asked if he wanted to switch seats, but he said no. Now outside of me and my son looking at each other every five minutes because we couldn't believe that we were sitting next to Dwight Howard, we kept our cool.

Anyway, as the service progressed, and we were instructed to "stand and grab your neighbor's hand, then lift that hand up" because you don't know what that person has been through. Now, I have to say this, I'm not sure if the man forgot that he was holding my hand, and I'm not sure if the man forgot that he was over six feet tall (and I'm five feet, three inches tall), but this man stretched my hand until I was on my tippy toes. And somehow, at the time I might add, I found it amusing as I looked at my son to see that he was watching. And with a whisper of slight concern he asked, "Are you okay?"

"Yes," I said as I shook my head in case he couldn't hear me.

"Does it hurt?"

"No, I'm okay." I assured him.

And the young man continued to hold my hand as I struggled on my tippy toes. For a split second I wondered, *is he doing this on purpose?* But then again, I wondered, *is he going through something and don't care that he has my hand stretched to the heaven?* But just as suddenly as the thought appeared, I realized what was happening in the natural was a reflection of what was happening in the spirit: *the Lord was stretching me.* And, therefore, I allowed Him to stretch me.

And a quick thought, *I'm in trouble* crossed my mind as the realization of the Lord getting ready to stretch me was before me.

And as I thought about being stretched, I was reminded of all that I had been through in the last seven years. I couldn't help but believe the Lord had been stretching me ever since. And immediately, the tears began to roll down my face as I was saturated with the goodness of the Lord's presence.

I took it all in as the Lord continued to minister to me. I stood before Him to minister to Him.

THE LORD SAID,

"I'M MOVING. TELL MY PEOPLE I'M MOVING."

And immediately, I knew the Lord was **DOING** something. He was about to **ESTABLISH** something. He was about to bring something forth; birth something. And my business is ringing in my spirit, so I knew He was doing something with my business. I continued to worship Him. As I sang unto Him, the Spirit gave me utterance, and I allowed Him to do whatever it was that He was doing. The tears continued to roll down my face as His presence overtook me.

As I stood before Him, He revealed that **I WAS ON ANOTHER LEVEL. MY FAITH WAS ON ANOTHER LEVEL.** I believed what He said about my business.

I AM AN ENTREPRENEUR.

And just as my faith grabbed a hold of what the Lord was saying, He continued to minister to me:

IN A VISION...

He reminded me of the vision of the fish, and He addressed my concern as I wondered *if the fish had been trapped or not...*

THE LORD SAID,

"**IT HAS BEEN CAUGHT. THIS ONE IS FOR YOU! NOW BE RESTORED."** And instantly **A VISION** of my business was before me. And revelation came forth: Your business was in germination. It was hidden. It was being developed. That's why you didn't have any clients. It wasn't that you couldn't get any clients – you weren't ready.

IT WASN'T TIME.

It had been ten years since the Lord had given me the vision:

THE WRITING ON THE WALL
PUBLISHING SERVICES

It had been ten years of me trying to establish the business. And every time someone came to me for business, *for one reason or another,* it didn't happen. And I couldn't understand why. But now I know; it was being developed. And now He was about to bring it forth. He was about to birth it forth.

THE LORD SAID,

"NOW YOU'RE READY!"

Now, I'm sure you already know, by that time, I was sobbing. I think "weeping" would be putting it too mildly. I was sobbing. The whole nine yards, snot and everything! I couldn't catch my breath, sobbing.

THE LORD WAS DOING THIS THING. IT WAS ABOUT TO COME FORTH. IT WAS ABOUT TO BE BIRTH.

And the **WORD OF THE LORD** rang out in my spirit, over and over, confirming what He was doing in my life:

THE LORD SAID,

"**ON ANOTHER LEVEL. ON ANOTHER LEVEL. ON ANOTHER LEVEL.**"

God is getting ready to do this thing on another level. It is getting ready to happen, on another level. It's going to be so much greater on this next level. This time is going to be so much greater than the first time. You tried it before, but...**ON ANOTHER LEVEL.**

ON ANOTHER LEVEL. ON ANOTHER LEVEL. ON ANOTHER LEVEL – I HEAR YOU GOD!

YOU ARE ON ANOTHER LEVEL!

YOUR FAITH HAS INCREASED AND PROPELLED YOU TO ANOTHER LEVEL!

FOR EVERYONE WHO ASKS, RECEIVES. EVERYONE WHO SEEKS, FINDS. AND TO EVERYONE WHO

KNOCKS, THE DOOR WILL BE OPENED.

LUKE 11:10 NLT

When we seek first the kingdom of God,
GOD IS FIRST IN OUR LIVES. HE is the focus of our
lives. HE is our source, and our resource. Our eyes
are stayed on Him. And thereby, as He blesses us,
He makes His command known:

TAKE SOME OF THE FIRSTFRUITS OF ALL THAT YOU
PRODUCE FROM THE SOIL OF THE LAND THE LORD
YOUR GOD IS GIVING YOU AND PUT THEM IN A
BASKET. THEN GO TO THE PLACE THE LORD YOUR
GOD WILL CHOOSE AS A DWELLING FOR HIS
NAME.

DEUTERONOMY 26:2 NIV

I understood. Unlike the tithe; a tenth of
what the Lord had blessed me with, the Lord
requires us to give Him the FIRSTFRUITS OF OUR
HARVEST. The firstfruits of a harvest is an offering
that is given unto to God, to thank Him for the
harvest. It's the firstfruit of our labor.

For example: To thank the Lord for blessing
you with the ingredients to bake a cake, you would

give Him the **WHOLE CAKE** as a firstfruits offering. *Then,* after you've *blessed Him first,* anything else you bake with the ingredients is yours. Therefore, in my case, *all of the financial resources* that I make from my *first client* will be my **FIRSTFRUIT;** offered unto the Lord in thanksgiving for the harvest. *And then the rest belongs to me!*

"YOU MUST NOT HOLD ANYTHING BACK WHEN YOU GIVE ME OFFERINGS FROM YOUR CROPS AND YOUR WINE.

"YOU MUST GIVE ME YOUR FIRSTBORN SONS.

EXODUS 22:29 NLT

Now, on the one hand, I'm thinking, *okay, that's on another level; I've never done that before.* But then, on the other hand, I'm excited in my spirit because **I KNOW THERE WILL BE A HARVEST!** Giving to God first out of what He has blessed us with demonstrates He's first in our lives.

"THE DAYS ARE COMING," DECLARES THE LORD,

"WHEN THE REAPER WILL BE OVERTAKEN BY THE PLOWMAN

AND THE PLANTER BY THE ONE TREADING GRAPES.
NEW WINE WILL DRIP FROM THE MOUNTAINS
AND FLOW FROM ALL THE HILLS,

AMOS 9:13 NIV

All I can say is, the fish is going to be so big, and the blessing is going to be so big that we are not going to be able to take it all in. We are not going to be able to handle it all – it's going to be so great. We are not going to have enough room to receive all that God has in store for us!

Get ready!

BUT I HAVE PRAYED FOR THEE, THAT THY FAITH
FAIL NOT: AND WHEN THOU ART CONVERTED,
STRENGTHEN THY BRETHREN.

LUKE 22:32 KJV

DAY 8

GIVE UNTO THE LORD THE GLORY DUE UNTO HIS NAME; WORSHIP THE LORD IN THE BEAUTY OF HOLINESS.

PSALM 29:2 KJV

As I go before the Lord, I hear a song in my spirit, and I welcome Him in. I started singing the song that the Lord had given me, and immediately I'm reminded of the prophetic dream that He had given me:

IN A DREAM...

I was at a worship service. The place was full to capacity; overflowing even. People were standing all around. I could see the entire place. And immediately, the presence of the Lord was overpowering. His presence filled the place, which was evident by all the people being overpowered by His Spirit. Evident by the people being slain in the

Spirit, weeping, and being healed as deliverance comes forth.

I stood watching in amazement. The anointing was so heavy in the place – you could feel it. It was almost as if you could cut it with a knife; it hung in the air, and made His presence known.

Then I noticed that the girl standing next to me was being "moved" by His Spirit. And when I went to lay my hands on her, she fell under the power of His Holy Spirit; slain in the spirit. Then, just as suddenly, the man standing on my left fell because he was slain in the Spirit as well.

My God!

And as I stood there,

THE LORD SAID,

"WHEN YOU WORSHIP ME, I WILL SHOW UP."

Not only is His presence there, but He shows up with power, healing, deliverance, whatever it is that you need; it's in His manifested presence. His anointing is present to meet *every* need.

Therefore, any and every time I look for the Lord's presence, I worship Him, and He shows up every time!

You want more of Him? You want to see Him increase in your life?

Worship Him!

HONOR THE LORD FOR THE GLORY OF HIS NAME.

FOR THEREIN IS THE RIGHTEOUSNESS OF GOD
REVEALED FROM FAITH TO FAITH: AS IT IS
WRITTEN, THE JUST SHALL LIVE BY FAITH.

ROMANS 1:17 KJV

DAY 9

...I WILL NEVER BE SHAKEN.

PSALM 62:2B NLT

Anxiously, I go before the Lord and await His presence. My soul has found rest in God. And in spite of the enemy's presence, I shall not be moved. I shall go before my God; My King. My soul shall not be cast down. My soul shall not be disquieted. My soul has found peace in His presence as I make my way before Him. I longed to go before Him. I longed for Him. He has kept me, and has made my footing sure.

For He has declared in His Word that I will never be shaken, and immediately, I am arrested in my spirit as I take hold, by faith, of the assurance of His Word.

I SHALL APPEAR BEFORE GOD.

In His presence, I praise and worship Him. And it doesn't take long for Him to reveal to me that I had been **WEAKENED** by the attack of the enemy, as **THE VISION** is before me to confirm what He said:

IN A VISION...

I saw a vulture, perched; waiting.

However, I continued to worship Him as His Holy Spirit encouraged me to press in. I continued to follow the Holy Spirit's lead and bless the Lord as the Spirit gave me the utterance to do so. And consequently, I was detained by the declaration and the decree that rung out in my spirit, over, and over, and over:

I WON'T BE SHAKEN.

I WON'T BE MOVED.

And although the enemy had come, I refused to be his prey. Even in my weakness, I declared that I would not be devoured. Therefore, I continued to press. Declaring, decreeing, and taking authority over the enemy.

MY SOUL RESTS IN GOD. MY SOUL HOPES IN GOD. MY SOUL TRUSTS IN GOD.

However, I couldn't help but be reminded of the Lord telling Peter that the enemy's desire was to sift Peter as wheat, as the vision of the vulture is before me. And it makes known the enemy's desire to sift me; shake me, move me…devour me.

AND THE LORD SAID, SIMON, SIMON, BEHOLD, SATAN HATH DESIRED TO HAVE YOU, THAT HE MAY SIFT YOU AS WHEAT:

BUT I HAVE PRAYED FOR THEE, THAT THY FAITH FAIL NOT: AND WHEN THOU ART CONVERTED, STRENGTHEN THY BRETHREN.

LUKE 22:31 – 32 KJV

Despite the fact that it was Satan's desire to sift Peter as a grain of wheat; in hopes of only finding chaff and be able to blow it away; in hopes that Peter's faith would falter. Like Peter, not only had my faith not faltered, but was in fact renewed; enhanced.

THE LORD'S PLAN HAD BEEN REVEALED WHILE I WAS IN THAT PLACE.

And it gave me clarity and understanding of what I had been called to do...in that place. He made known my **PURPOSE** for being in that place. And I was enlightened.

I CONTINUED TO PRESS IN.

I continue to bless the Lord in His Holy Temple. And shortly thereafter,

IN A VISION...

I saw the eagle rise up with his wings stretched out before me, soaring.

Again, I mount up. And immediately, I was strengthened.

I WON'T BE SHAKEN. I WON'T BE MOVED.

Though the fowler had come and the snares and traps were set, I wasn't moved. My hope is in thee Oh, Lord. Only you can save me. To God be the glory for the things He has done.

And while I remained in His presence, I continued to declare and decree my victory as I took authority over the enemy. My outlook had changed. I began to see things the way God saw them. And I rejoiced in the fact that the enemy could not overtake me.

I BELONG TO GOD. IN THEE OH, LORD, I PUT MY TRUST.

My soul finds rest in God alone; my salvation comes from Him. He alone is my rock and my salvation; He is my fortress. And it was only then, after I came into agreement with Him, that the Lord made known that **HE HAD GIVEN THE COMMAND...TO SHAKE ME:**

**"FOR I WILL GIVE THE COMMAND,
AND I WILL SHAKE THE PEOPLE OF ISRAEL
AMONG ALL THE NATIONS**

AS GRAIN IS SHAKEN IN A SIEVE,
AND NOT A PEBBLE WILL REACH THE GROUND.

AMOS 9:9 NIV

And yet, I rejoice in the shaking. For it was **IN THE SHAKING** the Lord's plan was revealed. It was **IN THE SHAKING** I learned **MY PURPOSE** for **BEING IN THIS PLACE.** It was **IN THE SHAKING** I learned **I WON'T BE SHAKEN. I WON'T BE MOVED.**

BUT THAT DOES NOT MEAN WE WANT TO
DOMINATE YOU BY TELLING YOU HOW TO PUT
YOUR FAITH INTO PRACTICE. WE WANT TO WORK
TOGETHER WITH YOU SO YOU WILL BE FULL OF
JOY, FOR IT IS BY YOUR OWN FAITH THAT YOU
STAND FIRM.

2 CORINTHIANS 1:24 NLT

DAY 10

AFTER THIS PRESENTATION TO ISRAEL'S LEADERS, MOSES AND AARON WENT AND SPOKE TO PHARAOH. THEY TOLD HIM, "THIS IS WHAT THE LORD, THE GOD OF ISRAEL, SAYS: LET MY PEOPLE GO SO THEY MAY HOLD A FESTIVAL IN MY HONOR IN THE WILDERNESS."

EXODUS 5:1 NLT

As soon as I woke up, the Lord invited me into His presence as the song of the Lord played in my spirit. I accepted His invitation, and sang unto Him. Now I'm not really sure, but I don't think I was able to get the first few words out before...

THE LORD SAID,

"TELL MY PEOPLE TO LET IT GO!"

And almost taken by surprise, my immediate reaction was silence – as I examined the words that were spoken. *Let it go?* Then I continued to praise Him as I waited for Him to give me understanding. And it wasn't long before He said, **"DAUGHTER,**

LISTEN" because my attention was divided. Not only was I trying to figure out, *what does He mean by, 'Let it go,' but also trying to quickly examine myself. Do I need to 'let something go?'*

I BECAME SILENT AS MY SONG CAME TO A HUSH, THEN SILENT.

I listened as the sound of the water from the fountain outside of my window fell like pouring rain. And all else around me was silent as well. HE HAD MY ATTENTION.

I was taken aback to find that He wanted to talk. So I lie prostrate before Him, and He continued:

THE LORD SAID,

"TELL MY PEOPLE TO COME BEFORE ME WITH THANKSGIVING; COME BEFORE ME WITH PRAISE. DON'T REHEARSE YOUR BITTERNESS IN MY PRESENCE. TELL THEM TO LET IT GO!"

And immediately I wondered, *what's going on?*

"**TELL THE ENEMY TO LET MY PEOPLE GO, SO THEY CAN WORSHIP ME,**" He continued. And immediately, I was prompted, and felt compelled to pray for the people; to intercede on their behalf. *Demanding that the enemy let the people of God go!*

As I had become concerned about the people of God, my heart searched for answers. And in His Majesty, He responded, "**THEY DON'T BELIEVE I CAN DELIVER THEM. THE OPPRESSION; THE ENEMY IS KEEPING THEM FROM BELIEVING. TELL MY PEOPLE TO WORSHIP ME. IF THEY WANT TO SEE ME MOVE IN THEIR LIVES, TELL THEM TO WORSHIP ME. TELL THEM TO MOVE ON. THEY CAN BE DELIVERED OR THEY CAN STAY STUCK. I'M DOING A NEW THING.**"

My heart was heavy for the people. And when He finished speaking, I started to pray.

As I remained in the Lord's presence, He revealed that while I was interceding, the people had to *want* to be set free. It wasn't just about the enemy letting the people go. The people had to *desire* to be free. They had to *want* to be delivered.

I sat before Him in awe. To see the goodness of our God, His heart being revealed. Even while we're in the wilderness, He provides for us. He takes care of us. He leads and guides us as the flock that we are.

BUT HE LED HIS OWN PEOPLE LIKE A FLOCK OF SHEEP,
GUIDING THEM SAFELY THROUGH THE WILDERNESS.

PSALM 78:52 NLT

It's amazing to just sit and think about just how good our God is. The fact that He loves us so much and wants desperately to see His people, His children, prosper that He reveals to us what's hindering us. He tells us what we need to do in order to receive the blessings. He doesn't want us to miss out on the blessings that He has in store for us!

HE WANTS TO BLESS HIS PEOPLE.

I continued to war and intercede as the Lord dictated; declaring and decreeing the freedom of

His people. Binding and loosing according to His word, and His instructions.

GOD IS SETTING HIS PEOPLE FREE!

Anyone who desires to be set free can be set free. God is the One who sets the captives free! It is by His hand that *the enemy is scattered!*

ALL WE HAVE TO DO IS DESIRE TO BE SET FREE. BELIEVE THAT HE WILL DO IT.

I continued to war: "I speak to the enemy right now, in the name of Jesus, and I command you to take your hands off of the people of God. Loose them! And let them go! In the name of Jesus! (And as the specific spirits were revealed, I casted them out; uprooted them.)

BE HEALED. BE DELIVERED. BE SET FREE. IN THE NAME OF JESUS!

COME OUT OF THE DARKNESS! COME OUT FROM AMONG THEM! AND SERVE GOD; THE ONLY TRUE AND LIVING GOD! WALK IN YOUR

AUTHORITY THAT GOD HAS GIVEN YOU! RISE UP
AND TAKE AUTHORITY! BE LOOSED! IN THE NAME
OF JESUS! TO GOD BE THE GLORY! NOW GIVE HIM
PRAISE!

As I prayed, the chains began to fall off of
the people of God! And I could see in the spirit that
the people started to believe. Their hope in God was
renewed. Their faith had increased. The people of
God were being set free from demonic oppression;
from strongholds.

THEN THE PEOPLE OF ISRAEL WERE CONVINCED
THAT THE LORD HAD SENT MOSES AND AARON.
WHEN THEY HEARD THAT THE LORD WAS
CONCERNED ABOUT THEM AND HAD SEEN THEIR
MISERY, THEY BOWED DOWN AND WORSHIPED.

EXODUS 4:31 NLT

I HAVE BEEN CRUCIFIED WITH CHRIST AND I NO
LONGER LIVE, BUT CHRIST LIVES IN ME. THE LIFE
I NOW LIVE IN THE BODY, I LIVE BY FAITH IN
THE SON OF GOD, WHO LOVED ME AND GAVE
HIMSELF FOR ME.

GALATIANS 2:20 NIV

DAY 11

AND SO, LORD, WHERE DO I PUT MY HOPE?
MY ONLY HOPE IS IN YOU.

PSALM 39:7 NLT

I was distracted by all that I had to do to get ready for our **FIRST WORSHIP SERVICE.** I was in awe of what God was doing; a promise being fulfilled. A promise that was, at one time afar off. A promise that I wasn't sure would ever be fulfilled.

And with that being said, my mind was blown that it was getting ready to actually happen. I couldn't help but think about all the times I **HOPED** someone would ask me to minister because I had **"A WORD."** I couldn't help but think about all the times I **HELPED** someone else with their ministry. I couldn't help but think about all the times I was **A PART OF** what someone else was doing in their ministry.

AND NOW, GOD WAS PREPARING ME FOR MY OWN.

I was no longer **WAITING** for someone to invite me to speak. I was no longer **"A PART OF"** someone's program. I was no longer **ASSISTING** someone with their ministry.

GOD WAS GIVING US, MY HUSBAND AND I, OUR OWN PLATFORM TO SPEAK FROM.

And now that time was upon us. God was getting ready to fulfill the promise that He made *by calling us into the ministry.* As I continued to praise and worship the Lord,

IN A VISION...

I kept seeing a rainbow appear before me.

And just as quickly as it appeared, it would disappear and another one would come. And this continued for a minute or so. **I KNEW IT WAS THE PROMISE OF GOD.**

GOD'S PROMISE WAS BEFORE ME.

Not only was it *a* promise, but *many* promises of God were about to be fulfilled. And, therefore, I continued to worship the Lord.

THE LORD SAID,

"TELL MY PEOPLE, THE TIME IS COMING; PREPARE. ALL THAT I HAVE FOR THEE I SHALL GIVE. YOU SHALL BE DELIVERED."

And immediately I was reminded of a woman who's pregnant.

THE LORD SAID,

"YOU SHALL BIRTH THE THINGS OF GOD. YOU SHALL STAND IN THE FEAT OF ADVERSITY. YOU SHALL DELIVER THE PEOPLE. YOU SHALL REIGN. YOU SHALL COME INTO ALL THAT I HAVE FOR YOU. EVERYWHERE YOUR FEET SHALL TROD YOU SHALL POSSESS THE LAND. YOU SHALL MOUNT UP WITH WINGS AS AN EAGLE AND POSSESS THE LAND.

I'M DOING A NEW THING. THE OLD HAS PASSED AWAY. I'M DOING A NEW THING. WATCH. I AM DOING A NEW THING. WATCH ME. AND SEE DON'T I PERFORM MY WORD. I AM HERE, DAUGHTER. DON'T BE AFRAID OF THE THINGS THAT YOU SEE. I AM HERE. I AM DOING A NEW THING. DON'T BE AFRAID OF THE THINGS YOU HEAR."

IN A VISION...

I see fire coming out of a house, out of the top floor windows. And although flames are coming out of the house, the house isn't burning. I see large flames of fire coming out of the windows. *I think there are two houses, but I'm not sure. It could be one house; a mansion maybe and it's just the way the house is structured.* The fire is coming out of the two windows in the one house and out of the one window of the other house.

THE LORD SAID,

"IT'S THE POSITIONING."

"I'M POSITIONING YOU AND RANDOLPH. YOU WILL BE FLAME THROWERS. FIRE. MY FIRE SHALL COME UPON YOU. MY PRESENCE SHALL COME UPON YOU. AND YOU SHALL DELIVER THE PEOPLE. AND NO ONE WILL BE ABLE TO PUT THE FIRE OUT. NO ONE WILL BE ABLE TO STAND IN MY PRESENCE UNCLEAN; NOT HOLY."

And suddenly,

IN A VISION...

I see a girl on the floor crying, sitting on the floor, crying as if deliverance is taking place. As if she desires to be made whole. She's crying out to God for deliverance.

THE LORD SAID,

"MY PRESENCE WILL DELIVER THE PEOPLE. GO, DAUGHTER. DO WHAT I'VE CALLED YOU TO DO. GO, DAUGHTER. SAY WHAT I'VE CALLED YOU TO SAY. THIS IS BETWEEN ME AND YOU; A COVENANT, TO DELIVER MY PEOPLE. CALL UPON ME AND I SHALL ANSWER. SEEK ME AND I SHALL

BE FOUND. COME TO ME AND WE SHALL BASK TOGETHER IN MY PRESENCE. I AM HERE. I WILL NEVER LEAVE YOU NOR FORSAKE YOU. DO MY WILL. LET MY PURPOSE BE YOUR FOCUS. NOT THE PEOPLE, ME. I'M YOUR FOCUS. AND I SHALL DELIVER THE PEOPLE. GREAT AND MIGHTY THINGS SHALL YOU DO. HEALING, DELIVERANCE. YOU SHALL BE CALLED MIGHTY; A MIGHTY WOMAN OF GOD.

HEAR ME DAUGHTER, MY FIRE SHALL RAIN DOWN ON YOU TO SET THE PEOPLE FREE. I AM PLEASED. COME BEFORE ME WITH THANKSGIVING AND PRAISE AND I SHALL APPEAR EVERY TIME.

NO LIMITS. NO LIMITS, DAUGHTER. NO LIMITS.

TELL MY PEOPLE TO GET READY. I'M DOING A NEW THING. GET READY. PREPARE."

"How? How shall the people prepare?" I asked.

"PRAISE AND WORSHIP," HE SAID. "I INHABIT THE PRAISES OF MY PEOPLE. I AM THERE."

Then all of a sudden, as I sat before the Lord, I was exhausted and could barely hold my head up. I was sooo exhausted – from being in His presence. And all I could think about was just getting back in the bed. I was exhausted! I took deep breaths to try to renew my energy. It was as if I had just run a race and had to try to catch my breath.

I WAS WEAK. I HAD TO LIE DOWN.

THE LORD'S VOICE WILL ROAR FROM ZION AND THUNDER FROM JERUSALEM, AND THE HEAVENS AND THE EARTH WILL SHAKE. BUT THE LORD WILL BE A REFUGE FOR HIS PEOPLE, A STRONG FORTRESS FOR THE PEOPLE OF ISRAEL.

JOEL 3:16 NLT

IN ADDITION TO ALL THIS, TAKE UP THE SHIELD
OF FAITH, WITH WHICH YOU CAN EXTINGUISH ALL
THE FLAMING ARROWS OF THE EVIL ONE.

EPHESIANS 6:16 NIV

DAY 12

THEN JESUS SAID TO THE DISCIPLES, "HAVE FAITH IN GOD.

MARK 11:22 NLT

As I sung unto the Lord, I heard in my spirit *the blessing is already yours.* And I continued to worship the Lord as the realization of this thing became clear; **IT'S ALREADY DONE.** And I thought about the ministry. **IT'S ALREADY DONE. IT'S MINE. THE PROMISE BELONGS TO ME.**

THE LORD SAID,

"I'VE ALREADY GIVEN IT TO YOU."

As I allowed the word of the Lord to resonate in my mind, I couldn't help but wonder, *had I been praying about something that had already been done? Had I been asking for something that had already been done? Had I wanted God to do something for me that had already been done?* And just as suddenly, I was reminded that the contract had already been signed. The day we signed the contract was the day the blessing became a reality.

ARE WE WAITING FOR GOD TO DO SOMETHING THAT HAS ALREADY BEEN DONE? ARE WE PRAISING HIM IN EXPECTATION FOR SOMETHING THAT HAS ALREADY BEEN DONE? ARE WE PRAYING FOR SOMETHING THAT HAS ALREADY BEEN DONE?

I was in awe as I continued to praise and worship the Lord. I was amazed.

IT'S ALREADY DONE!

WHILE YOU WERE SLEEPING, GOD WORKED IT OUT FOR YOU.

I don't know what you're facing. I don't know what you're dealing with. I don't know what you're afraid of, but,

THE LORD SAID,

"IT'S OVER!"

And when God says, "It's over!" It's over!

As I stood on my balcony, I watched the fish in the lake. One of the fish was in a sand bank that it had obviously prepared over time. This, for the most part, is where it was all day every day. I could see him take a mouthful of sand from inside the hole and put it outside the hole. And immediately I thought *he's working.* And for a quick second I wondered *if* **WE'RE** *continuously working to get something that we already have in an attempt to make it bigger, deeper, or wider. A better fit. Better accommodation.* Then…

THE LORD SAID,

"STOP TRYING TO MAKE THE BLESSING HAPPEN. IT HAS ALREADY HAPPENED."

I understand there are some people who are trying to work for the blessing:

And immediately I was reminded of a time when my husband and I wanted to *bless* our son with our car, so that he could get back and forth to school. However, we still had a small balance on the car that we had to pay off before we were able to *bless* him with the car. However, in his excitement to get what we were trying to *bless* him with, he said he'd pay the small balance off. Unfortunately, my husband wasn't in agreement because he said, "If he pays the balance off, then it's not a *blessing.* In essence, he bought the car for the small balance that was left on the car."

WE'RE TRYING TO WORK FOR SOMETHING THAT GOD IS TRYING TO GIVE US.

WE'RE TRYING TO PAY FOR SOMETHING THAT GOD IS TRYING TO GIVE US.

You see, our son didn't want to wait for the blessing. He wanted it right then and there. He wanted it to accommodate himself, to make it more convenient for himself. And of course, I said all of that to say that some of us may be doing the same thing and don't know that's what we're doing. And this is to let you know – that's what you're doing. And if you want the blessing from the Lord, you'll have to wait for it. You can't pay the balance off yourself. You can't make it happen for yourself because you're inconvenienced.

OTHERWISE, IT'S NOT A BLESSING. YOU BOUGHT IT.

Otherwise, you've just made a **DECISION:** purchased a car, and called it faith.

Allow me to say this: **FAITH IS NOT A QUICK DECISION. IT'S NOT A SPLIT DECISION.**

FAITH DOESN'T WORK OVERNIGHT, AND IT ISN'T INSTANT.

You see, Randolph and I believed God for fourteen years that He'd give us our own ministry to pour into the lives of the people. And now, it has finally happened. God has given us **THE EMBASSY OF GRACE.** Now I didn't say that to say because it took us fourteen years that it'll take the next person fourteen years. But **I DID** say that to say:

FAITH WAITS ON GOD. FAITH HOPES IN GOD. FAITH BELIEVES IN GOD.

Faith, like a seed, is planted in your spirit. And just like any other seed that is deposited into your spirit, it has to take root, grow, develop; mature over time. And over that time, it waits on God. It hopes in God. It believes in God. And it's only *after* our faith has matured, that we're able to receive the fruit of our labor; **THE PROMISE.** It's only *after* our faith is matured that we receive the **THING** that we've been hoping, praying, believing for.

Allow me to use the analogy of an expectant mother. The **BABY** is a picture of **FAITH** working: growing, developing, depending on the mother for everything that he needs. It works in secret. It works in the hidden place where no one sees it growing, developing, maturing. But **YOU KNOW** it's growing and developing as **THE DAY OF EXPECTATION** approaches. And the closer you get to **THE DUE DATE** the better prepared you are to receive the blessing.

You see, not only is the baby (your faith) being developed, but **YOU ARE BEING DEVELOPED** as well. You're growing and maturing as well. So that when that day comes, **YOU'RE PREPARED; YOU'RE READY** for what God has for you; **THE BLESSING.**

And just like the baby, who depends on his mother to provide everything that he needs, faith depends on God to provide everything that it needs.

FAITH IS IN GOD

THE LORD SAID,

"FAITH IS <u>IN</u> ME."

And immediately,

IN A VISION...

I saw His glory just hovering over my head and then filled the room. Faith in Him **IS** being in His presence as His Holy Spirit envelops us, and takes us into His Holy place, and we become one with Him.

SO YOU HAVE TO BE **IN** GOD TO GET FAITH

FAITH IS **IN** HIS PRESENCE.

FAITH IS **IN** WHO HE IS.

Now just as my spirit is IN me, faith is IN Him. That means HE IS FAITH. HE IS whatever it is that you want or need. So does that mean He's a car? No, it means He's your Provider who'll give you the car. He's your Healer who'll give you the healing that you need. He's your Deliverer who'll give you the deliverance that you need.

Faith is **NOT** in the **THING** you want Him to provide.

Faith is the **EVIDENCE** of the thing that you had been **HOPING** for. So when you get the **THING** that you had been hoping for, it is **EVIDENCE** that you used your faith to get it.

NIGHT AND DAY WE PRAY MOST EARNESTLY THAT
WE MAY SEE YOU AGAIN AND SUPPLY WHAT IS
LACKING IN YOUR FAITH.

1 THESSALONIANS 3:10 NIV

DAY 13

IN THE DAYTIME HE LED THEM BY A CLOUD,
AND ALL NIGHT BY A PILLAR OF FIRE.

PSALM 78:14 NLT

As I praised the Lord,

IN A VISION...

I saw **HIS GLORY APPEAR IN A CLOUD; HIS
MANIFESTED PRESENCE.**

And I knew He was there, and I was in His
presence. So I continued to worship Him and
welcome Him in.

As the vision was before me, I couldn't help
but be reminded that it was His presence *in a cloud*
that led the children of Israel. And immediately, I
was assured that His presence would lead and guide
me. And immediately,

I SAW FIRE.

HE MADE HIS PRESENCE KNOWN.

I have been entrusted to care for His people. And suddenly, I'm not really sure of what I've signed up for, as I'm reminded of the dream I had several months ago: **I HAD THE CROSS ON MY BACK, IT WAS HEAVY.** And the desire to usher the people into His presence challenged my ability to lead this people.

The ever so **SLIGHT, BUT I KNOW IT'S THERE** anxiety; apprehension of my ability. I try to comfort myself as I remind myself that this would be the first time I was on my own.

NO PRAISE TEAM, NO PRAISE LEADER, NO VISITING CHOIR, NO PSALMIST, AND NO SOLO ARTIST.

I desired nothing more than to lead them into His presence, as He prepared their hearts to receive Him.

HE ANSWERED MY HEART'S CONCERN.

THE LORD SAID,

"MY DAUGHTER, I SHALL LEAD YOU AND
YOU SHALL FOLLOW ME. JUST SAY WHAT I TELL
YOU TO SAY, AND DO WHAT I TELL YOU TO DO. I
WILL GIVE YOU WISDOM."

I was comforted as I relinquished the NOTION
that somehow I was the one doing the leading. I
rested in knowing that HE would lead HIS own
people. And even so, I couldn't help but to be
reminded of Solomon, who, undoubtedly, felt the
same way I did. Or should I say, I felt the same way
he did:

GIVE ME AN UNDERSTANDING HEART SO THAT I
CAN GOVERN YOUR PEOPLE WELL AND KNOW THE
DIFFERENCE BETWEEN RIGHT AND WRONG. FOR
WHO BY HIMSELF IS ABLE TO GOVERN THIS GREAT
PEOPLE OF YOURS?"

1 KINGS 3:9 NLT

Wisdom is seeking God. Wisdom belongs to
God.

THE LORD SAID,

"WISDOM IS MINE."

THESE ARE THE PROVERBS OF SOLOMON, DAVID'S SON, KING OF ISRAEL.

THEIR PURPOSE IS TO TEACH PEOPLE WISDOM AND DISCIPLINE,
TO HELP THEM UNDERSTAND THE INSIGHTS OF THE WISE.
THEIR PURPOSE IS TO TEACH PEOPLE TO LIVE DISCIPLINED AND SUCCESSFUL LIVES,
TO HELP THEM DO WHAT IS RIGHT, JUST, AND FAIR.
THESE PROVERBS WILL GIVE INSIGHT TO THE SIMPLE,
KNOWLEDGE AND DISCERNMENT TO THE YOUNG.

LET THE WISE LISTEN TO THESE PROVERBS AND BECOME EVEN WISER.
LET THOSE WITH UNDERSTANDING RECEIVE GUIDANCE
BY EXPLORING THE MEANING IN THESE PROVERBS AND PARABLES,
THE WORDS OF THE WISE AND THEIR RIDDLES.

FEAR OF THE LORD IS THE FOUNDATION OF TRUE KNOWLEDGE,
BUT FOOLS DESPISE WISDOM AND DISCIPLINE.

PROVERBS 1:1 – 7 NLT

WE OUGHT ALWAYS TO THANK GOD FOR
YOU, BROTHERS AND SISTERS, AND RIGHTLY SO,
BECAUSE YOUR FAITH IS GROWING MORE AND
MORE, AND THE LOVE ALL OF YOU HAVE FOR ONE
ANOTHER IS INCREASING.

2 THESSALONIANS 1:3 NIV

DAY 14

DON'T WORRY ABOUT ANYTHING; INSTEAD, PRAY ABOUT EVERYTHING. TELL GOD WHAT YOU NEED, AND THANK HIM FOR ALL HE HAS DONE. THEN YOU WILL EXPERIENCE GOD'S PEACE, WHICH EXCEEDS ANYTHING WE CAN UNDERSTAND. HIS PEACE WILL GUARD YOUR HEARTS AND MINDS AS YOU LIVE IN CHRIST JESUS.

PHILIPPIANS 4:6 – 7 NLT

I woke up this morning after an amazing, much needed, night of peaceful, restful sleep.

So when I went before the Lord in song, I have to say that I was at peace. I was confident and sure that everything was going to be all right. And as I worshiped, I noticed the Lord was silent. Therefore, I looked for Him, and welcomed His presence. And He assured me.

THE LORD SAID,

"I'M HERE."

It was almost as if I had nothing to say because I was so peaceful. I almost wanted to take the Lord's lead and just be quiet. Somewhere between the day before, me being extremely stressed out, and waking up this morning, I decided that the things that concerned me yesterday were not going to concern me today. There was no point in worrying about what has already been done.

You see, I believe that when the Lord told me that 'He has already given it to me; that it's already done,' that everything that's **CONNECTED** with the promise is *also* already done: The people He has ordained to be a part of the ministry. How the praise and worship will be conducted. How the order of service will go. **EVERYTHING! ALREADY DONE!**

Therefore, I'm not going to worry about what is already done. I **WILL** do as the Lord said, **'PREPARE.'** But I'm not going to worry about it. I'm not going to worry about if anyone will show up. I'm not going to worry that we don't have our name on the building - none of it! I'm just not going to worry about it. It's already done. Those whom the Lord has chosen and ordained to be a part of this ministry will be there. And if not on the first day, then they're coming.

THE MINISTRY BELONGS TO GOD. IT'S HIS MINISTRY. THEY ARE HIS PEOPLE. AND THEREFORE, I'LL LET HIM TAKE CARE OF HIS PEOPLE; HIS BRIDE.

I'M GOING TO LET GOD BE GOD.

And while He's being God, I'll encourage myself with some **LEFTOVERS** that He has given me. I will encourage myself (as David said), as I'm reminded of what the Lord has done for me: We've had prayer gatherings and our prayers were answered. We've had praise and worship gatherings and didn't have a praise team or a psalmist but we sang our hearts out to the Lord. We've had bible study and didn't have a huge crowd. And guess what? He showed up! He was there every time! I remember, in spite of all the attempts that I made to get the people to come and join us, the ones the Lord had **ORDAINED** to be a part of the ministry were there. **AND THAT'S ALL THAT MATTERS.**

THEN YOU WILL EXPERIENCE GOD'S PEACE, WHICH EXCEEDS ANYTHING WE CAN UNDERSTAND. HIS PEACE WILL GUARD YOUR HEARTS AND MINDS AS YOU LIVE IN CHRIST JESUS.

I really felt at a loss for words. I don't know what else to say. When we take our focus off Jesus and become consumed with what's going on around us, it is *then* that the fear, worry, doubt, anxiety, apprehension comes in. Therefore, let us keep our eyes stayed on Jesus, and He'll give us the peace we need that passes, or exceeds anything that we can understand.

Whenever you start to worry, stop and pray.

God's peace is different from the world's peace (John 14:27). True peace is not found in positive thinking, in the absence of conflict, or in good feelings. It comes from **KNOWING** that God is in control. Our citizenship in Christ's Kingdom is sure, our destiny is set, and we have victory over sin. Let God's peace guard your heart against anxiety.

"I AM LEAVING YOU WITH A GIFT—PEACE OF MIND AND HEART. AND THE PEACE I GIVE IS A GIFT THE WORLD CANNOT GIVE. SO DON'T BE TROUBLED OR AFRAID.

JOHN 14:27 NLT

God has given us a gift – peace of mind and heart.

PEACE. BE STILL.

Then I was reminded of what the Lord has done in my life, and with each step of the way I've found comfort in knowing that **I'VE BEEN HERE BEFORE ALTHOUGH IT'S NOT LIKE BEFORE.** In other words, I've already had a glimpse of what this is all about. I've already experienced this before on a somewhat smaller level. This isn't the first time that I've been introduced to what the Lord is doing in my life…although now it is a little different.

While I've never been responsible for having a "Sunday Worship Service," I have had prayer, praise and worship, bible study, which is somewhat on a smaller scale. Then I remind myself I'VE TRAINED FOR THIS. THIS IS WHAT ALL OF THE YEARS OF TRAINING WAS FOR.

I AM ON ANOTHER LEVEL NOW.

THE LORD HAS FOUND US FAITHFUL AND HAS ENTRUSTED US WITH MORE.

FIGHT THE GOOD FIGHT OF THE FAITH. TAKE HOLD
OF THE ETERNAL LIFE TO WHICH YOU WERE
CALLED WHEN YOU MADE YOUR GOOD
CONFESSION IN THE PRESENCE OF MANY WITNESSES.

1 TIMOTHY 6:12 NIV

DAY 15

DO NOT DESPISE THESE SMALL BEGINNINGS, FOR THE LORD REJOICES TO SEE THE WORK BEGIN,...

ZECHARIAH 4:10 NLT

As I went before the Lord in song, I continued to rest in His peace. And as the day of **NEW BEGINNINGS** approached, I have to say that at that point, I wasn't afraid. When I thought about the word of God that's mentioned above, I got excited in my spirit. Not only is this a very familiar scripture, which can more than likely be quoted by most, if not all, Christians. But it is a very powerful scripture that I believe most people fail to heed.

- ❖ Yes, powerful; we are **NOT TO DESPISE THE SMALL BEGINNINGS.**
- ❖ Yes, powerful; we are to **BE FAITHFUL** over what the Lord has entrusted us with
  - ○ Even if it seems small and insignificant to others.

❖ Yes, powerful; the small beginnings are a testament to what the Lord is doing in our lives.

❖ Yes, powerful; we are to do everything that we can do
  ○ For the people of God.

❖ Yes, powerful; that we'll see what God is capable of doing; His end results,
  ○ His blessings.

❖ Yes, powerful; we are to rejoice because a day will come when the Lord will cause the small beginning to become enlarged.

However, what I want to focus on today is the fact that THE LORD REJOICES to see the work begin.

NOW THAT'S POWERFUL!

The Lord rejoices to see the work begin. As I meditated on this scripture, my spirit got excited when the Lord revealed to me that **HE WAS CELEBRATING** with us; He was celebrating because He sees us getting started with the work; the ministry. Now you should be just as excited about your own situation that you believe God for.

THE LORD IS CELEBRATING US GETTING STARTED WITH THE MINISTRY.
HE IS EXCITED ABOUT, REJOICES IN, COMMEMORATES, HONORS WHAT WE'RE DOING.

He is looking down from heaven, taking note of what we're doing. And He's going to honor the work of our hands. Wait! I shouldn't say, going to, He has already honored the work of our hands. He said, 'Already; it is already done.' He has already blessed us for doing the work; for starting the work. And we rejoice in knowing that some of those blessings will manifest on the first day that we start the ministry. I cannot wait to see the blessings of the Lord!

How could anyone think that they could do something for God and He doesn't bless you? I'm excited even now to know that the Lord is going to bless what we're doing. I'm excited to know that He will honor us for the work we're doing.

IN EXCHANGE, I REJOICE IN WHAT THE LORD IS DOING, AND GETTING READY TO DO.

And suddenly, the realization of what's getting ready to happen is revealed to me:

THE LORD IS GETTING READY TO BLESS US! THERE IS A BLESSING WAITING FOR US!

How can we *think* that we are going to come together to celebrate the Lord for what He has done, and He doesn't bless us?

WE ARE CELEBRATING HIM! WE ARE CELEBRATING WHO HE IS! WE ARE CELEBRATING WHAT HE HAS DONE! WE ARE CELEBRATING HIM FOR PUTTING US IN THE MINISTRY!

I *imagine* that just as we are waiting, anticipating the day to come, and filled with expectation that the Lord is in heaven waiting, anticipating the day to come, and filled with expectation as well, so that He can pour our His blessings upon us! **HE IS JUST AS EXCITED AS WE ARE.** We can't forget about:

THEN HE SAID TO ME, "THIS IS WHAT THE LORD SAYS TO ZERUBBABEL: IT IS NOT BY FORCE NOR BY STRENGTH, BUT BY MY SPIRIT, SAYS THE LORD OF HEAVEN'S ARMIES.

ZECHARIAH 4:6 NLT

It is only by His Spirit that we're going to be able to do the things that He has called us to do. It doesn't matter how much effort we put forth, it doesn't matter how much work we do, it is only by His Spirit that it will come to pass. Therefore, as you live for God, determine not to trust in your own strength or abilities. Instead depend on Him and work in the power of His Spirit!

I was weakened in His presence. I tried to stand, but stumbled as the words rung out in my spirit and I cried out, "Lord! We stand in awe of your glory!" And the tears rolled down my face as I wept before Him. I was drained. I had no strength left. And that in itself was enough for me. It was enough to know that we are headed in the right direction. And with that being said, we rejoiced as well. And we do not take this assignment lightly; to shepherd God's people.

AND THE SPIRIT OF THE LORD WILL REST ON
HIM—
THE SPIRIT OF WISDOM AND UNDERSTANDING,
THE SPIRIT OF COUNSEL AND MIGHT,
THE SPIRIT OF KNOWLEDGE AND THE FEAR OF
THE LORD.
HE WILL DELIGHT IN OBEYING THE LORD.
HE WILL NOT JUDGE BY APPEARANCE
NOR MAKE A DECISION BASED ON HEARSAY.
HE WILL GIVE JUSTICE TO THE POOR
AND MAKE FAIR DECISIONS FOR THE EXPLOITED.
THE EARTH WILL SHAKE AT THE FORCE OF HIS
WORD,
AND ONE BREATH FROM HIS MOUTH WILL
DESTROY THE WICKED.

ISAIAH 11:2 – 4 NLT

I PRAY THAT YOUR PARTNERSHIP WITH US IN THE
FAITH MAY BE EFFECTIVE IN DEEPENING YOUR
UNDERSTANDING OF EVERY GOOD THING WE SHARE
FOR THE SAKE OF CHRIST.

PHILEMON 6 NIV

DAY 16

I was anxious to get into the Lord's presence, but was met with many distractions. My spirit longed to go before the Lord. And I tried to figure out when I would appear before Him. When would I find the time? Then, finally, the time came. Saddened; that there wasn't a song in my spirit. However, as soon as I entered into my secret place, the Lord spoke into my spirit,

THE LORD SAID,

"GREATER IS COMING!"

And immediately, I started to rejoice in the word of the Lord. I knew the Lord was preparing me for greater! It's a new season!

I couldn't help but wonder, as my spirit searched for meaning, if His promise was as a result of yesterday; seeing the place where we were going to have the service. In spite of the small beginning, He has promised that greater is coming!

REMAIN FAITHFUL OVER THE LITTLE.

I had hope that *this too* shall come to pass. As He has always done, He's going to enlarge our territory. He's going to give us more! He's going to bless us with more; abundance!

IN A VISION...

I see the Lord coming in the clouds; the Lord coming in great power.

I received His power in my spirit. And immediately, I was reminded of our instruction to pray: *Thy Kingdom come...*

THY KINGDOM COME, THY WILL BE DONE IN EARTH, AS IT IS IN HEAVEN.

MATTHEW 6:10 KJV

And immediately, I was taken aback at the revelation of God coming into the world to express Himself with power, and to assert His power over the enemy; Satan. **HIS WILL** to be done in my life, through obedience, as He leads and guides me.

FOR THE SAKE OF HIS PEOPLE.

FAITH IS THE CONFIDENCE THAT WHAT WE HOPE
FOR WILL ACTUALLY HAPPEN; IT GIVES US
ASSURANCE ABOUT THINGS WE CANNOT SEE.

HEBREWS 11:1 NLT

DAY 17

FOR THIS IS WHAT THE LORD, THE GOD OF
ISRAEL, SAYS: 'THE JAR OF FLOUR WILL NOT BE
USED UP AND THE JUG OF OIL WILL NOT RUN
DRY UNTIL THE DAY THE LORD SENDS RAIN ON
THE LAND.'"

1 KINGS 17:14 NIV

As I go before the Lord in song, I am
distracted. And yet, I try to press my way. Even as I
continue to sing unto Him, He's silent.

And while the glory cloud has appeared, I
feel prompted to pray; so I prayed. As I pray,

IN A VISION...

God was pouring a pitcher of water onto a
table. The oil overflowed and went over the edge of
the table.

Immediately, I wondered why there wasn't a
VESSEL that He was pouring into. *What does the
vision mean?* I wondered. Then suddenly...

THE LORD SAID,

"NOT A SINGLE GLASS..."

Then suddenly, several tall glasses were lined up one next to another. They were about thirty-two ounces each, filled with water. I noticed that as they were lined up, the count continued to increase so that I could not see where they ended. And immediately, I was reminded of the widow whose *flour and oil* would never run out because she believed the Lord. And I rejoiced in the Lord as the vision was before me.

THE LORD SAID,

"I CANNOT BE CONTAINED."

THE INTERPRETATION OF THE VISION...

The Lord was pouring Himself out.

And consequently, I understood why there wasn't a *vessel* for Him to pour into. There isn't a "single" vessel that can contain Him, which explains why the glasses were continuous and I couldn't see the end;

He's endless.

As He continued to reveal Himself to me, I became desperate for Him. And immediately, the song in my spirit changed as I cried out before Him. I longed for Him. I wanted more of Him.

BUT WHEN YOU ASK HIM, BE SURE THAT YOUR
FAITH IS IN GOD ALONE. DO NOT WAVER, FOR A
PERSON WITH DIVIDED LOYALTY IS AS UNSETTLED
AS A WAVE OF THE SEA THAT IS BLOWN AND
TOSSED BY THE WIND.

JAMES 1:6 NLT

DAY 18

DO NOT DESPISE THESE SMALL BEGINNINGS, FOR
THE LORD REJOICES TO SEE THE WORK BEGIN,

ZECHARIAH 4:10 NLT

Zechariah chapter four, verse ten was the scripture we chose to focus on for our first Sunday Worship Service. It had also been determined that rather than a regular Sunday Worship Service, the *first* Sunday was going to be a celebration unto the Lord, and therefore, both Randolph and I would minister the word of God.

So when the Lord invited me into His presence for my 3 a.m. devotion, I was excited to see what He had to say. I asked the Lord, "What do you want me to say to the people of God?" So, I want to share with you what the Lord wanted me to share with the people of God:

SMALL, BUT MIGHTY!

In April 2000, I had a dream:

IN THE DREAM...

I saw an office. The office was empty, but I knew by the furniture in the office that it had to be the office for the president of the company. It was a *really* nice office. The desk, credenza, filing cabinets, all made of mahogany or cherry wood; you knew the furniture was expensive.

I saw balloons in the office; therefore, I knew there was some sort of celebration. And the Lord said, "Promotion." And immediately, in my spirit, I knew that this was MY office, and that I was being promoted.

Then I woke up.

I was excited, of course, to know that God was getting ready to promote me! God was getting ready to bless me! After all, I had spent ten years working for that company – and now I was being promoted. However, in spite of the promotion, I was disturbed in my spirit. I couldn't seem to figure out the prestige of the office because the president's office in the company wasn't as prestigious as the one I saw in the dream. So this promotion was higher than the president in the company. It baffled me, and yet, I hung on to the word of the Lord. I hung on to the promise of God. I knew God was getting ready to promote me!

When I got to work the next day, I was in my office when my manager called me and asked if I would meet him in Human Resources (H.R.) in about ten minutes or so. I was like, "WOW God! This is getting ready to happen!" While I had been a manager for about two or three years, I had only been in *that* particular position for about a year. And just as equally amazing, I had been getting promoted every year.

THE PROMOTIONS CAME AND SO DID THE CHALLENGES.

Anyway, I went over to H.R., my manager and the H.R. Specialist were already there. After I sat down and got settled in my seat, my manager advised me that I was being let go. He went on to say that because I had been **SHARING THE GOSPEL** they had to let me go. Immediately, I rose up from my seat, getting ready to snap, I mean, defend myself when the angel that stood beside me put his hand on my shoulder and I sat back down. I didn't say anything.

It was over! There was no defending myself! There was no defending the gospel!

My assignment on that job was over.

So, I extended my hand and thanked them for the opportunities that I had been afforded, and I left.

Now, on my way back to my office, I ran into a co-worker who pulled me to the side. "I have to tell you something," she said. "While you were out on vacation, George was going around asking all of the other managers if they had heard you sharing the gospel. And while I don't know what the other managers said, I told him, 'No, I hadn't heard her sharing the gospel.'"

"Girl," I said laughing. "Where were you ten minutes ago?"

"Why?"

"I just came back from H.R. They let me go for 'sharing the gospel.'"

"They did!" she gasped. "Daisy, that's not right. I'm telling you, George was looking for a reason to fire you, but you see he couldn't come up with anything but you were sharing the gospel. That's okay. That just means your assignment here is up."

"You're right." I said. "My assignment here is up."

I went home, wondering *what did the dream mean?*

After several months of being home, somehow, some way, Randolph and I were led to a church that took us an hour to get there and an hour back to our home. But it was in that place that we started our ministerial training. And after three intense years of training, we were licensed as Ministers of the gospel. Then after another year of intense training, we were ordained.

And along the way, I wrote my first book, *The Ties That Bind.* I shared how the Lord healed, delivered, and set me free from the hurt and pain I suffered for twenty-years as a result of an ungodly soul-tie; an unhealthy relationship. And it was then that Randolph and I went from city to city, state to state preaching the gospel. Preaching at women's conferences, retreats, men's conferences and in the prison (my husband went to the prison – I wasn't going to the prison).

Deliverance session after deliverance session, invitations to come here to speak, invitations to go there to speak, to make my book available to the men and women of God; who by the Lord's anointing healed, delivered, and set free those who read the book, who were bound.

We continued to preach on a consistent basis at the church we belonged to.

And along the way, the Lord entrusted Randolph and I to start our own ministry, which we did. As well as having our own broadcast on the radio.

WE REMAINED FAITHFUL.

Then after years of us being stretched with full-time ministry, I went back to work, only to find that the housing market had collapsed. And Randolph was working at the Post Office when the Lord challenged him: If you want an ordinary life, I'll give it to you. But if you want an extraordinary life, I'll give *that* to you, as well. In which he responded, "I want an extraordinary life."

Then the Lord prompted us to move to Orlando, Florida.

And challenged us to give up everything that the Lord had blessed us with: The house that we believed for, the car that we believed for, the family and friends, who were our only support, and the church that had become our pillar. Somehow, someway, we believed the blessings of the Lord were in Orlando, Florida. So, we rented our house, sold our car, said good bye to our family and friends, and packed up and came to Orlando with no money, no jobs, no family, and no friends.

We had only one purpose for coming to Orlando and that was: to start the ministry.

As the tears rolled down my face, I was reminded of the impact that the transition made on our lives. We were in a foreign land. But along the way, we got jobs, where promotions came quickly. We got friends, and family came quickly.

And along the way, I was prompted to start a prayer group on the job, which I did.

Along the way, I was prompted to have praise and worship gatherings in our home, which I did.

Along the way, Randolph and I were prompted to have bible study in our home, which we did.

Along the way, I wrote my second book *Birthing Ministry; Leadership Essentials* as I labored to birth the ministry that the Lord had given us. I continued to cry before the Lord as I was reminded that in the book, I talk about my experience of hurt, pain, and betrayal that comes with birthing a ministry; starting a ministry.

And I talked about the *essential leadership skills* that are required if you covet this office.

And along the way, the Lord began to prompt us to start our ministry, which we did. We started our radio broadcast, "A Set Time."

Along the way, the Lord revealed that it was time to begin the work. It was time to begin building the Temple. And on December 31, 2013, my assignment on that job was over.

And on April 2014…

- Fourteen years after having the dream, "We are living that dream."
- Fourteen years after seeing the office, "We are standing in that office."
- Fourteen years after receiving the promise of God, "We are preaching the gospel of Jesus Christ.

THIS OFFICE is the highest office any man can obtain – promotion comes from God."

Therefore, I want to encourage you today. What you may be doing for the Lord may seem small. What you're going through on account of the Lord's leading may seem insignificant. But I'm telling you THE LORD REJOICES TO SEE THE WORK BEGIN.

You may not be building the Temple as in the church, but you may be building your *temple*. Our bodies are the *temple* of the Holy Spirit. You may think that growing in the things of God is small and insignificant, but the Lord rejoices to see the work begin.

HOW FOOLISH! CAN'T YOU SEE THAT FAITH
WITHOUT GOOD DEEDS IS USELESS?

JAMES 2:20 NLT

DAY 19

Instantly something like scales fell from Saul's eyes, and he regained his sight.

ACTS 9:18A NLT

I couldn't stop the tears from falling from my eyes as I sat in the Lord's presence.

I was sorrowful. I was distressed. I was regretful.

I woke up that morning to the voice of the Lord telling me to "RISE UP." And immediately, I knew He wasn't telling me to *rise up* as in *get out of bed*, but rather, He was telling me to rise up in my spirit; TAKE AUTHORITY!

IT WAS TIME TO FIGHT; I WAS IN WARFARE.

But my spirit was so weighed down, that I found it difficult to not only rise up, but to even get up out of the bed. I knew I was supposed to pray;

not only pray but take authority! I had to do it! I had to go before Him in order to get the help that I needed for the fight. But I couldn't get up!

Not only was I weighed down in my spirit, but my eyes were so tired and sleepy that I could barely open them. I knew the Lord was present. Therefore, I mustered up as much strength as I could and just started declaring my victory in the Lord. I commanded the enemy to take his hands off of me, so that I could be free. And I started to war right there as I lie in the Lord's presence.

The heaviness that was in my spirit gave way to my displeasure of the outcome of the invitations that were sent out for our *first* Sunday Worship Service Celebration.

I WAS STRUGGLING WITH MY FAITH.

And immediately,

THE LORD SAID,

"YOU'RE FISHING IN THE WRONG POND."

And in a whisper, I ask, as my spirit was still distraught, "Where shall I let down my net? Where are the fish? Show me, Lord; tell me, where are the fish?"

And suddenly,

IN A VISION:

I saw a radio. And the times 3:15 and 7:15 appeared before me. And immediately I knew that it was an indication of our radio broadcast, "A Set Time." I found comfort in knowing that the people who the Lord had ordained and appointed to be a part of this ministry were the people who listened to our radio broadcast.

I WAS STRENGTHENED BY HIS WORDS.

Once I was strengthened, I got up and went into my secret place, and began to war in the spirit. Again, commanding the enemy to loose not only me, but the people of God that He had appointed to be a part of the ministry. I declared and decreed in the spirit, that they would come, and called them forth.

As I continued to pray, war in the spirit, whatever the Lord revealed to me that was what I warred against. As I was praying,

IN A VISION...

I saw an eye with a scale on it.

And immediately, I began to pray that the scales would fall from the eyes of the people. I also prayed that the scales would fall from *my* eyes, and immediately, the scales fell from my eyes, as the Lord spoke...

THE INTERPRETATION OF THE VISION...

Instantly, **THE EYES OF MY UNDERSTANDING** were opened. And just as suddenly, I understood that the people who I invited to be a part of the worship celebration were not appointed to be a part of this ministry, which is why He said I was "fishing in the wrong pond."

He also revealed that I had the wrong focus. While I was focused on *the people,* that wasn't *the purpose.* In essence, I lost sight of the vision; the purpose for us inviting the people. While it was a celebration unto the Lord – it was not a celebration because the people were coming.

SO WHY WAS I DOWNCAST BECAUSE THE PEOPLE WEREN'T COMING?

I was inviting friends; the people I knew. When God was saying, the appointed people are *a people that we don't know, nor have we ever seen.* There's nothing wrong with inviting friends, but we have to be lead by the Spirit. Go where He's telling us to go. Do what He's telling us to do.

Are we looking for "friends" or are we looking for people who are appointed to help with the work?

Do you have **VISION** or are you using your **SIGHT** to see what God sees?

THESE TRIALS WILL SHOW THAT YOUR FAITH IS GENUINE. IT IS BEING TESTED AS FIRE TESTS AND PURIFIES GOLD—THOUGH YOUR FAITH IS FAR MORE PRECIOUS THAN MERE GOLD. SO WHEN YOUR FAITH REMAINS STRONG THROUGH MANY TRIALS, IT WILL BRING YOU MUCH PRAISE AND GLORY AND HONOR ON THE DAY WHEN JESUS CHRIST IS REVEALED TO THE WHOLE WORLD.

1 PETER 1:7 NLT

DAY 20

"BE STRONG AND COURAGEOUS,..."

JOSHUA 1:6A NLT

As I went before the Lord in song, my only focus was to praise Him. There was a new song in my spirit. I followed the Holy Spirit's lead, and sang as He revealed the song me:

WE WELCOME YOU IN, HOLY SPIRIT.

Immediately, I felt the Lord's anointing, and I knew He was present. I continued to welcome Him.

As I continued to follow the Holy Spirit's lead, I praised and worshiped Him – in song.

I have to say, I was excited because of the reservations for the worship celebration. A person that I least expected has accepted my invitation to join the worship celebration. In my spirit I was thanking the Lord that while my focus was in the wrong place, He was gracious enough to allow this individual to come.

So, my efforts weren't all for naught. I was just spending too much time in a place that wasn't *effective.* Anyway, as the anointing increased, my spirit began to weep before Him in *thanksgiving.*

Somehow, I still couldn't believe this was really getting ready to happen! We were about to start our own ministry! And I was in awe of what God was doing. And immediately,

THE LORD SAID,

"LISTEN TO MY VOICE. LISTEN TO MY VOICE.

I AM WITH YOU. I WILL GO BEFORE YOU. I WILL BE THERE. I WILL MAKE THE CROOKED WAYS STRAIGHT, EXALT THE LOW PLACES, AND BRING DOWN THE HIGH PLACES. I WILL TEACH YOU. I WILL SHOW YOU WHAT TO DO. DO NOT BE AFRAID."

All I could do was praise Him; worship Him and sing unto Him in song.

This thing that you've been praying for; this thing that you've been believing for; this thing that you've been fasting for; this thing that you've dreamed of – is getting ready to happen!

BE THANKFUL FOR WHAT THE LORD HAS DONE.

BE THANKFUL FOR WHAT THE LORD IS DOING.

BE THANKFUL FOR WHAT THE LORD IS GETTING READY TO DO.

BE STRONG AND COURAGEOUS.

GOD SAVED YOU BY HIS GRACE WHEN YOU
BELIEVED. AND YOU CAN'T TAKE CREDIT FOR THIS;
IT IS A GIFT FROM GOD. SALVATION IS NOT A
REWARD FOR THE GOOD THINGS WE HAVE DONE,
SO NONE OF US CAN BOAST ABOUT IT.

EPHESIANS 2:8-9 NLT

DAY 21

THEREFORE, SINCE WE ARE SURROUNDED BY SUCH
A GREAT CLOUD OF WITNESSES, LET US THROW
OFF EVERYTHING THAT HINDERS AND THE SIN
THAT SO EASILY ENTANGLES. AND LET US
RUN WITH PERSEVERANCE THE RACE MARKED OUT
FOR US,

HEBREWS 12: 1 NIV

It was the day the Lord had made:

The first day "the doors of the church"
opened.

THE EMBASSY OF GRACE

Nothing but excitement on one hand, and
nervousness on the other, hung in the air. It was all
surreal. I couldn't believe that it was really
happening. My old, faithful words play over and
over in my mind: **I'VE BEEN HERE BEFORE, BUT IT'S
NOT LIKE BEFORE.** Well, technically, we had never
been in *that* place before. Now that I think about it.
The Lord had never told us to start a ministry. Start

the ministry; start bible study, but He has never said, "Start the church; start building the Temple." So we were actually standing on unfamiliar territory. Although it felt somewhat familiar, it was not familiar at all.

When we thought about the reality of it all, we were amazed: We are starting our own church. We weren't guest speakers for anyone else's ministry. We weren't helping build someone else's ministry. And it wouldn't be a one-shot deal. In fact, it was the beginning of many shots to come.

As we prepared to get ready, frantic that we would forget something, we went over the checklist again and again. All was accounted for.

Then Randolph received a text message from his brother in Chicago, wishing us well on our first Sunday Service. And immediately, the text message stirred up emotions that caused memories of their mother, who was no longer with us, to surface.

We were finally ready to leave. Somehow the "more than enough time" had turned into "on the verge of running late." We had to set up: the banner, balloons, CD player, and the laptop to record the service. (Maybe that was a lot to try to do on the first day, but we did it.)

I thought about the last few days, and how I had peace. Peace that passed all understanding. I couldn't seem to figure it out, and it didn't seem to make any sense. I was about to embark on one of the greatest days of my life, and nothing. Peace. Any other time, had I been invited to be the guest speaker for someone, or was participating in a church function of any kind, I would have been extremely nervous. With all sorts of thoughts running through my head: *Am I ready? Had I prepared enough? What are the people going to say? Am I open to hear from God?*

Surprisingly, there wasn't any nervousness at all; none whatsoever. So I braced myself for the *calm before the storm.* I had pretty much reasoned that once we were at the church somehow, someway, all hell was going to break loose.

As we were driving to the church, again, I was all calm, cool, and collected. Then suddenly, out of nowhere,

IN A VISION...

I SAW MY MOTHER; APPEAR IN THE CLOUDS, LOOKING DOWN FROM HEAVEN WATCHING ME.

And immediately, the tears started to flow from my eyes. Quickly, I tried to catch the tears before they fell onto my blouse. But my swiftness was no match for the quickness of the tears as they made their way down my face and dripped not only onto my blouse, but my jacket as well.

It was *then* that I knew, without a shadow of doubt, **I WAS WALKING IN MY DESTINY. I KNEW THIS WAS WHAT I WAS CALLED TO DO. I WAS WALKING IN MY PURPOSE.**

I couldn't really describe what it felt like to not only SEE my mother, but to know that she was WATCHING over me. Almost as if the Lord was saying, SHE WAS FRONT AND CENTER to cheer me on. She was there. And the weird thing was (when I thought about it) it had always been somewhat irritating when I heard people say, "Mom, I know you're watching this." Or "Grandma, I know you're looking down from heaven…" as they looked up to heaven. Now I can say, "I know exactly what they mean."

THEREFORE, SINCE WE ARE SURROUNDED BY SUCH A GREAT CLOUD OF WITNESSES, LET US THROW OFF EVERYTHING THAT HINDERS AND THE SIN THAT SO EASILY ENTANGLES. AND LET US RUN WITH PERSEVERANCE THE RACE MARKED OUT FOR US,

HEBREWS 12: 1 NIV

It was overwhelming to say the least. It was almost as if the Lord said, *"I have a surprise guest for you."* It was truly a blessing. I understood that she couldn't be there if the Lord wasn't there, so it went without saying that He, too, was watching.

Going into the service I was what Randolph and I call "full." The slightest move of God and the tears would come bursting forth.

We made it to the place and unloaded the car. Hurried in to set up and finished just as the first guest was arriving. And again, *to my surprise,* it was a friend of mine, who I had no idea was coming. It was a blessing to see her and her husband.

I couldn't write this *faith walk* without saying, "My desire was that the place would be jammed packed." You see, my challenge during these *21* days was to stretch my faith. Increase my faith. Stretch it beyond normal limits to receive the blessings God had in store for me. So to believe beyond normal limits meant, the room jammed packed and standing room only…in my mind. And words could not express how anxious I was to get to that day to *see* just what the Lord had done; the miracle He had performed. The *fish* He brought out of the pond.

We started the service by welcoming everyone to *The Embassy of Grace, our first Sunday Worship Service.* We had time for praise and worship, then two of our friends shared words of encouragement, and so did I. And of course, we honored the Lord with our giving, and Pastor Randolph delivered the Word of God. Our *only concern* was if the Lord was pleased, which we knew He was as His anointing rested in the place. We were excited about our first Sunday service…and the five people who came to celebrate with us.

As the day wore on, my every thought was of seeing my mother. And every time I thought about the Lord's goodness and Him allowing my mother to be there, it was just overwhelming. And the tears would come bursting forth each time I thought about seeing her. It was amazing. I mean, words couldn't really describe how much it meant to me, but God knew.

Sometimes, when we're looking for that someone; sometimes, when we're looking for that support – that someone to be there for us – God knows who we need; He knows who that someone is. And He'll send them just when you need them, even if He has to open up the heavens for you to see them.

And still the Lord's peace hung onto to me like wings of a dove.

"I KNOW ALL THE THINGS YOU DO. I HAVE SEEN YOUR LOVE, YOUR FAITH, YOUR SERVICE, AND YOUR PATIENT ENDURANCE. AND I CAN SEE YOUR CONSTANT IMPROVEMENT IN ALL THESE THINGS."

REVELATION 2:19 NLT

EPILOGUE

The blessings of the Lord came quickly, and by faith, I grabbed a hold of everything that He was doing.

THINK BEYOND THE FOUR WALLS OF THE "CHURCH;" BELIEVE BEYOND NORMAL LIMITS.

It may not look like what you've prayed for, but God has answered your prayer. Think beyond what you're used to; believe beyond the limits. Think outside the box; do something that you've never done before! **OPEN YOUR EYES AND SEE WHAT THE LORD HAS DONE!**

Expect God to do the impossible. Expect Him to do beyond anything that you can imagine or think.

The encounters that I've had with God have been nothing short of absolutely amazing; mind-blowing, unlike anything that I've experienced before. Somehow, someway, I've found that I've been able to TAKE HIM AT HIS WORD like never before. I mean, when He says it, swoosh; I GRAB A HOLD OF IT. And *that thing* is in my spirit until it comes to pass!

The Lord has so graciously blessed me with the opportunity to write five books (since writing my first book, *The Ties That Bind*), which allows me to share my faith and my experiences. It also allows me to do *ministry* in the written form of God's word; reaching people that may never, otherwise, come to one of our "church" services or may never hear the sound of my voice.

He has also blessed me with a blog website: *The Ties That Bind* that also allows me to minister in written word, beyond the four walls, which I invite you to be a part of: tiesthatbinddd.wix.com/tiesthatbind.

We have an outreach ministry that goes beyond the four walls to evangelize and minister; meet the "spiritual" needs of the people, pray for people, their salvation, and minister in the gifts of the Holy Spirit. The outreach allows us to give back to the community, which we do by having Thanksgiving Turkey Giveaways and Christmas Toy Drives (for example).

The borders of my women's ministry have been enlarged as a result of God so graciously enlarging my territory; by expanding my women's ministry to Orlando, Florida. It has now become one ministry in two locations: one in Chicago, IL and one in Orlando, FL, (which is a bi-lingual, Spanish speaking ministry).

The Lord has opened so many doors for us that we can't really name them all.

And I believe that like the woman whose *cruse of flour and jar of oil* will not run out; neither will God's blessing, as long as I continue to stretch my faith; believe beyond normal limits! To God be the glory for the things He has done! Stretch Your Faith! Be Blessed!

WE HAVING THE SAME SPIRIT OF FAITH,
ACCORDING AS IT IS WRITTEN, I BELIEVED, AND
THEREFORE HAVE I SPOKEN; WE ALSO BELIEVE,
AND THEREFORE SPEAK;

2 CORINTHIANS 4:13 KJV

ABOUT DAISY S. DANIELS

Daisy S. Daniels has been married to Randolph E. Daniels, Sr. for 23 years. They have three children: Ronald, DaiSha, and Randolph, Jr. Daisy is Pastor of The Embassy of Grace (co-laborer with Senior Pastor, Randolph Daniels).

Prophetess Daisy's leadership, motivational, and transformational expertise encourages, inspires, and empowers the body of Christ.

She is founder and CEO of Daisy S. Daniels Ministries; a ministry that empowers women to increase in mind, body, soul and spirit to break spiritual, physical, psychological, emotional, and sexual strongholds.

She is President and CEO of The Writing on the Wall Publishing Services; a full-service Christian publishing house that is committed to excellence in Christian-theme publications that enables you to write and publish the books of your dreams.

She received her M.B.A. in International Business from Keller Graduate School of Management in 2011.

TO CONTACT THE AUTHOR

Write: Daisy S. Daniels
    P.O. BOX 621433
    Orlando, FL 32862
Telephone: (708) 704-6117
Email: daisysdaniels@aol.com
Website: www.daisysdaniels.wix.com/ministry

ALSO BY DAISY S. DANIELS

THE TIES THAT BIND

BIRTHING MINISTRY

INCREASE!

BREAD FROM HEAVEN

YOUR FAITH IS ON TRIAL

THE WRITING ON THE WALL PUBLISHING SERVICES

The Writing on the Wall Publishing Services is a Christian publishing house that is committed to excellence in Christian-theme publications. Our goal is to equip you with the tools needed to successfully write, publish, and print your intellectual property, which will allow you to minister to the nations and advance the Kingdom of God. Our services include:

* MANUSCRIPT REVIEW
* EDITING
* MANUSCRIPT DEVELOPMENT / CONSULTING
* PAGE DESIGN AND LAYOUT
* COVER DESIGN
* ISBN NUMBER / BOOKLAND EAN BARCODE
* PRINTING
* COPYRIGHT

For more information, contact us:

Write: The Writing on the Wall Publishing Services
P.O. BOX 621433
Orlando, FL 32862 – 1433
Telephone: (708) 704-6117
Email: thewritingonthewall@aol.com
Website:
www.thewritingonthewal.wix.com/daisysdaniels

www.ingramcontent.com/pod-product-compliance
Lightning Source LLC
LaVergne TN
LVHW051056080426
835508LV00019B/1912